I touch your things. I sit in your chair. I lie on your bed. You can't see me – but I can see you.

Illustration by Kelly Renee Schutz

Paranormal Encounters
Manifestations

FIRST EDITION
"Book 9"

Dr. Kelly Renee Schutz
Author

Cover Designer and Illustrators

Cover/Back:	Brandy Woods	Canada
Illustrations:	Brandy Woods	Canada
Illustration:	Magdalena Adic	Croatia
Illustration:	George Patsouras	New York
Illustration:	Katie Wheeler	Minnesota
Photographs:	Kelly Schutz	Minnesota

Published by: Paranormal Universal Press, LLC
Coon Rapids, Minnesota 55448
www.paranormaluniversalpress.com
Email = krschutz1@yahoo.com

Printed by: CreateSpace, an Amazon.com Company

Paranormal Encounters
Manifestations

All images, cover art, illustrations, and text are copyrighted under the laws of the United States of America.

Copyright © 2019 by Dr. Kelly Renee Schutz and Paranormal Universal Press, LLC. All rights reserved.

This book, or parts thereof, may not be reproduced or transmitted in any form without the express permission from the publisher, Paranormal Universal Press, LLC and author. The author acknowledges United States copyright protections of intellectual property as well as international copyright laws and its guiding rules.

Correspondence and Book Orders
Paranormal Universal Press, LLC
krschutz1@yahoo.com

ISBN: 978-1-79413-414-0

Printed in the United States of America

Disclaimer

This is the ninth book written in the Paranormal Encounters series. Book 9 is a compilation of all stories as copied from Books 3 (technically Books 1-2) and 5. Not included in this book are topics from Book 4 (Defying Naturalism) or several experiences as encountered by children (Book 6 - Through a Child's Eyes). Book 7 (Paranormal Phenomena) provides a broad summary of all stories from Books 1-6. Book 8 (Investigative Journal) is useful when ghost hunting.

The study and exploration of paranormal phenomena brings with it much excitement, speculation, and ridicule. Those who have not had an experience with the paranormal are often quick to judge with certainty that such phenomena do not exist. Some non-believers feel those exploring the unknown are tampering with demonic energies.

To date, the author continues to experience and investigates unexplained paranormal events while sharing her viewpoints on her top ranked show, Paranormal Encounters Podcast Series (currently ranked 1-4 worldwide). Link to her show can be found on website: **www.paranormaluniversalpress.com**. Subscribing and downloading podcast segments is free.

Paranormal Encounters: Manifestations shares true encounters as experienced by the author and guests. Pioneers in the field who make it their life mission to understand this phenomenon convey similar experiences with similar energies. Which lends itself to the question – at what point will we, as investigators, begin to experience energies that are <u>not</u> so common?

Stories are illustrated with sketches to help the reader visually experience situations from the author's perspective. Sketches are modified to protect the anonymity of physical locations, situations, and people. Images or stories resembling your own encounters, situations, or actual persons - known, living, or dead - are coincidental.

This book is intended as a form of entertainment. The stories shared in this book are not exaggerations or made up accounts of encounters experienced in unexplained situations. Most stories do not involve a demonic encounter. Rather, these negative or perceived to be demonic encounters illustrate various forms of paranormal energy.

Properties mentioned in this book are either private property or are advertised to the general public as being haunted. The author makes no representations or claims as to the accuracy of their "being haunted."

However, the author does believe each of her personal encounters involved unexplained paranormal activity. While it is exciting to explore and capture paranormal activity, a beginning ghost seeker should always take proper steps to respect private property while adhering to trespassing laws.

Always seek permission when exploring private property.

Dedications

I would like to dedicate this book to my husband, family, friends, and those who share my passion in exploring the paranormal field. My motivation in trying to find answers to my unexplained encounters is often put to task by scientific laws of naturalism.

I would also like to thank my husband for his tolerance in my enthusiasm in chasing ghosts by spending most of our vacations at haunted locations so I could use him as "ghost bait" to help me determine whether paranormal events do exist.

Finally, thank you to the little girl and older man, who I photographed in the lower window screen at what was once my father's – grandfather's and built by my great grandfather's home on May 6, 2007 (image in this book). The clarity of their features along with their expressions of puzzlement in looking at me sparked a question in my mind to revisit the genealogical research I had written about them in my family history. This error of "identity" has since been corrected.

Capturing their images not only turned my disbelief about ghosts into the realization that some not only exist but live (visit) in their former homes or places of comfort sharing messages with us by manifesting from beyond the grave.

A special thank you to my illustrative team - Brandy Woods (cover designer and illustrator, Canada), Magdalena Adic (former cover designer and illustrator, Croatia), George Patsouras (illustrator, New York), and Katie Wheeler (illustrator, Minnesota) for helping me visually tell my personal, real-life stories.

Table of Contents
Manifestations

Illustration by Magdalena Adic

Table of Contents

Disclaimer. iii
Dedications v
Author, Cover Designer, Illustrators x
Introduction 1
Investigation Preparation Log 8
Protection Prayers 9

BOOKS 1 and 3 – Titles From These Books
Chapter 1: Behind the Curtain 18
Chapter 2: Ouija Board – "Butter Damn'it" 35
Chapter 3: "Bring It On" – Rubber Ducky 42
Chapter 4: Clinking Coins – Ghost Maid 59
Chapter 5: Kicked in the Air 78
Chapter 6: Choked in Bed 88
Chapter 7: Voices – The Love Affair 98
Chapter 8: Ectoplasmic Orbs – Nanny-Kids 105
Chapter 9: The Farmstead Children 115
Chapter 10: Book Flying Off Shelf 127
Chapter 11: Attacked by a Jealous Woman 136
Chapter 12: Haunted Marbles 143

BOOKS 2 and 3 – Titles From These Books
Chapter 13: Get Off Of My Back 154
Chapter 14: Pennies and Pillow Cases 163
Chapter 15: Faces in the Window Screen 169
Chapter 16: Haunted Classroom 181

Table of Contents
(continued)

BOOKS 2 and 3 (continued)
Chapter 17: Dance Manifests Music 190
Chapter 18: Visitors in the Barn 196
Chapter 19: Silent Night, Holy Butterfly 203
Chapter 20: Orbs Relaying Messages 215
Chapter 21: Tomatoes Jumping Off Shelf 231
Chapter 22: Haunted Pioneer Saloon 239
Chapter 23: The Basement Ghost 272
Chapter 24: Dark Shadow 283

BOOK 5 – Best Titles From This Book
Chapter 25: Looking Blue Today 290
Chapter 26: C-r-e-e-e-k 296
Chapter 27: Artwork Not For Sale 304
Chapter 28: Guardian Angel? Uh, No............... 308
Chapter 29: Cowboy in the Cabin Window 314
Chapter 30: Haunted Las Vegas Hotels 321
Chapter 31: Prince Rupert Hotel 333

Book Covers 368
Podcast Series – Music Composers and Voice Talent .. 376

- Author -
and
Illustrative Designing Team

AUTHOR   COVER/BACK

ILLUSTRATORS

Author
Dr. Kelly Renee Schutz

Dr. Kelly Renee Schutz specializes in applied communications and human behavior. Her lifelong interests have included understanding differences among people with a secondary interest in exploring paranormal phenomena. She holds four advanced degrees. A former legal investigator, she uses intuition and common sense to guide her in understanding unexplained situations. Dr. Schutz is a writer, former college instructor, former paralegal investigator, professional photographer, crafter, auction enthusiast, world artist, and world traveler. She has three small businesses (Artisan Impressions, LLC, Farmhouse Confectioneries & Dough, and Paranormal Universal Press, LLC). She hosts and produces "Paranormal Encounters Podcast Series" as heard on Podomatic and thru Para-X Radio Network (top ranked). She is involved with Fine Art America. Website: **www.paranormaluniversalpress.com**.

Cover Artist and Illustrator
Brandy Woods, Canada

Brandy Woods is an award-winning visual illustrator who specializes in Native American-inspired and fantasy themes. She enjoys painting and sculpture. While she doesn't personally have status, a distant grandmother was full-blooded Choctaw and she was raised with a deep love and respect for the First Nations. She graduated with honors from Dawson College's prestigious Illustration and Design program. She grew up in Louisiana and spent much of her childhood reading Wendy Pini's 'ElfQuest', as well as numerous books on mythology, shamanism, fantasy, and other cultures. She has long dreamed of illustrating books, to inspire a new generation of dreamers. Brandy was contracted for this multi-book project to showcase her life-sketching talents. Recommended artist of **upwork.com**. Here work can be seen at **www.brandywoods.com**.

Illustrator (Sketch)
George Patsouras, New York

George Patsouras currently lives in Long Island City, New York. He began developing his artistic skills at a very young age. As a child, he was inspired to draw everything from comics to Greek Mythology. Then, his favorite medium was using pencils. Now, an established artist, he combines a variety of media techniques using pencils and digital painting. A freelance artist (with much success), he has risen to becoming established in illustration arts. Many of his works can be seen on numerous publications – ranging from board games to card games. His work can also be seen on various book covers. George loves what he does and it shows in personal artistic style. George was contracted to prepare an illustrative sketch for this book. He is a recommended artist of **upwork.com**.

Illustrator (Sketch)
Katie Wheeler, Minneapolis, Minnesota

Katie Wheeler was born in southern Minnesota. She is currently studying architectural design in the College of Design at the University of Minnesota, Minneapolis. She would consider herself to be a visual artist who likes to illustrate using oils, paints, acrylics, and pencils. At the age of five years old, she began working with paints and pencils discovering her love for art. Bringing her images to life, she has provided sketches for two books, one that is a personal biography and the other, a published book made into a series. Her artwork has been sold as greeting and notecards in hobby stores as well as a contribution to raise money to help kids afford art supplies at a premier art gallery near Chicago, Illinois. Katie likes to listen to music, travel, and go to art museums. She is working on her design portfolio while attending design school.

What Not To Say To A Ghost
"Bring It On"

Illustration by George Patsouras

Introduction

This is Book 9 in the Paranormal Encounters series. It contains a compilation of all stories as written in Books 1-3 and 5, as well as includes bonus chapters from those books.

My having a discussion with people about ghosts brings many types of responses. Reactions have varied from fear to disbelief regarding their existence and is often followed by one of these comments, "if ghosts exist, then, why haven't I seen or encountered one?" "Where is this ghost in which you speak of?" "Here, ghostie, ghostie, ha-ha." Or, "I think you need to see a shrink because your brain cells are malfunctioning – he-he." I learned a long time ago that it is pointless to try to convince someone who has never had a paranormal encounter that ghosts do exist. Some people have experiences and some do not. When the time comes, you will know and will not doubt.

The subject of ghosts is not a "top five" water cooler topic either. Have you ever heard someone say during a lunch break, "so, was your pesky ghost behaving itself last night?" or "Full moon tonight – BOO." Most people are uncomfortable discussing this topic and have tendencies to change the subject quickly by ignoring it, expressing a reaction, or remaining silent. In a verbal poll I conducted a few years ago amongst a diverse group of people, it was found that about 84% not only believed in ghosts but felt they had a personal encounter with one. About 11% were skeptical about them but expressed their being afraid to experience an event for fear of encountering something demonic. And, about 5% felt ghosts did not exist concluding in their minds that the stories people shared were either made up in their heads, imagined, or contrived.

Why do some people have experiences and others do not? This is not an easy question to answer. My responses generally lean in the direction of sensitivity, timing [chance], ignoring cues, attitude about them, environmental and weather conditions, moon phases, or personal beliefs about the afterlife.

It is RARE that one can easily "call out" or "see" a ghost on verbal request. On occasion, I have had this ability to do so given the right conditions. However, many people are not so fortunate to experience a ghost, leading to disappointment or the questioning of their existence. If a floor squeaks, does this mean a ghost is present? Maybe this sound is an imprint or is due to a temperature change in the environment. A wall bangs or knocks ... does this mean a ghost is trying to gain your attention? Or, maybe the pipes are expanding and clanking. A dead clock hands move to different times of the day during new and full moon phases. Is this a battery malfunction, weather change, or home electrical emittance issue? Could any of these situations mean a ghost is present? Possibly.

Those who are overly sensitive often have what is called a *sixth sensory sense*. A *sixth sensory sense* is best described as a psychic radar (more sensitive to the observation of cues) that most people do not readily see or just ignore. High frequency. Most would agree that watching for or paying too much attention to unusual cues in their surroundings is not only exhausting but a waste of time and energy often leading to a form of paranoia. Trying to summon a ghost can lead to energy drain.

Since the age of eight, I have been aware I have a *sixth sensory sense*. Today, I would just tell you that my frequency is higher than most. You may have heard about situations of children playing with an imaginary friend. I never had such a playmate but my husband did at the age of 3. Children are very sensitive and intuitive before the age of 6. Although their abilities are more sensitive around this age, it is not uncommon to hear that experiences also occur between the ages of 6-12.

At age 3, my husband played alone most of the time. One day, his mother asked him who he was playing with, to which he responded, "Bob." It just so happens he had a deceased brother by the name of "Robert" [passed away before he was born] however, the name of this child was never revealed to him until age 50. It was by accident he found out his brother's name when he overheard a conversation between his mother and myself (mumbling in the kitchen). Coincidence? Perhaps. It is more likely that he was playing with his deceased uncle, also named Robert, who was his mother's brother.

Nevertheless, not all imaginary play friends are "ghost" encounters. Not all children see or have ghost playmates. In most cases, parents believe their child will grow out of their imaginary play friend stage as they get older because a child's sensitivity to cues in their surroundings desensitize over time.

My fascination with the afterlife grew to a heightened level after the discovery of my photographing two ghost faces in the upper window screen of my former grandparents' house on May 6, 2007. This image appears in this book. On this day, my attitude about whether ghosts existed changed.

Before this date, I would have unexplained moments of anxiousness in situations causing me distress or stomach aches (often passed off as hormonal changes or depression).

At an early age, I was never a fan of going upstairs alone, opening closed doors, walking down into dark basements, etc. I have no idea why. Not alone in feeling this way, my young nephew refused to go into his home basement by himself or into my grandparent's barn (haunted) that can be viewed from 150 feet away from the house (very haunted). When asked why not, he has a hard time explaining his resistance and just simply refuses. Is he experiencing a "sixth sensory sense" or are these situations just "unfamiliar"?

In my teens, I continually wished I could see a ghost. People always talked about them, but I felt I wasn't fortunate enough to have an experience. My wish to see a ghost (relayed out loud while walking alone on my grandparent's property in my young teens) came without warning on May 6, 2007 (not sought out).

The home, built by my great grandfather and passed down to my grandfather and father, survived a straight-line tornado force wind that ripped through the property knocking over a 150-year old tree onto a live powerline. This weather event not only shook the house but caused a manifestation of who I believe are two of my deceased family members in a screened window. In doing research, the young gal, believed to be my great aunt, died in their first of four homes two miles away. The older man, believed to be my great grandfather, passed away in a hospital but had a strong attachment to this home and property.

My great grandparents had lived in three homes in the same area before building their fourth home, a very grand home, with his own hands in the early 1900's. The day I visited the property (post-tornado), it had not occurred to me that I was being watched by someone[s] in an upper screened window. On this day, the weather conditions were overcast, a bitterly cold feeling resonated throughout the air, still breeze, birds chirping, and the sound of an electrical charge radiating from the downed tree onto a powerline and into the air. A limestone foundation under the home acted as a conductor for creating energy, possibly charged from the storm's lightning strikes. What I did not realize then was that these conditions became the perfect recipe for manifestation of visible anomalies. Electricity is an energy source needed for manifestations.

Most ghost hunting enthusiasts know the five basic rules: (1) protect yourself (wear or hold a cross and say a protection prayer), (2) show respect to the deceased, (3) understand your reasons for seeking ghosts, (4) know when to leave them alone, and, (5) respect private property. It is best to ask for permission before entering a premise. It can be quite exciting to capture a paranormal anomaly; but do so with good practice, not wrong practice.

From personal experience, ghosts come and leave quickly, often working on their own schedules. Most visual manifestations (orb, mist, appearance) lasts 3-5 seconds. Ghosts generally reveal themselves to one person, not to pairs or groups. A ghost's cooperation with you will depend on a variety of circumstances as well as their comfort in being around you.

I would not consider myself to be psychic. I would call myself a sensitive intuitive (empath) who is able sequence together unexplained coincidences or cues when given a situation where someone who has passed presents messages to me. My being open about their existence is what attracts them to me with 99.5% of my experiences being non-threatening.

Although the goal of this book is to entertain and share with you my personal real-life stories, it is also designed to give further insight into paranormal topics, help you become a better observer when investigating unexplained situations, and offers theories that typically defy the laws naturalism.

Experiencing a paranormal event can happen at any age and can be life changing. For some, it's thrilling – for others, it's terrifying. Whether you are a believer or not ... here is where your journey about this phenomenon either evolves or ends.

Dr. Kelly Renee Schutz

Books Written

BOOK 1
Paranormal Encounters: Attacks, Manifestations, Attachments, Poltergeists [Topics and Illustrated Personal Real-Life Stories]

BOOK 2
Paranormal Encounters: Be Careful What You Wish For [Topics and Illustrated Personal Real-Life Stories]

BOOK 3
Paranormal Encounters: Beyond the Grave [Non-Fiction, Stories Compiled from Books 1 and 2]

BOOK 4
Paranormal Encounters: Defying Naturalism [Topics Only]

BOOK 5
Paranormal Encounters: Hanging Around [Non-Fiction and Fiction Paranormal Stories]

BOOK 6
Paranormal Encounters: Through A Child's Eyes [Non-Fiction, Fiction - Children's Perspectives and Adult]

BOOK 7
Paranormal Encounters: Haunted Phenomena [Non-Fiction, 70+ Stories Compiled from Books 1-6 - Shortened]

BOOK 8
Investigative Journal

Investigation Preparation Log

- ☐ Research of the location completed. Interviews of the subjects completed.

- ☐ Received permissions to go onto the location or site.

- ☐ Assembled a small investigation team.

- ☐ All equipment fully charged with back-up accessories.

- ☐ Understands hazards involved. Bring face masks for poor air quality or molds; wear proper footwear and jacket. Etc.

- ☐ All to be wearing a holy cross. Say protection prayer. Be conscious of unusual physical reactions.

- ☐ Bring notebook or audio recorder to take notes to debunk situations and record unusual events.

- ☐ Bring trigger objects if you intend to use them.

- ☐ Your software is advanced enough to review EVPs or watch video tapings for analysis.

- ☐ Follow-up with client to review findings or set up another time for a 2nd or 3rd investigation of location.

Protection Prayers

ALWAYS PROTECT YOURSELF
When spirit adventuring, it is important you wear or carry a cross or religious/spiritual object, say a protection prayer, and surround yourself with white light to create a safety shield from harmful entities. Say prayer before bedtime in haunted location.

SIGN OF THE CROSS with or without HOLY WATER
"*In the name of the Father and of the Son and of the Holy Spirit. Amen.*" Dabble water on forehead, dabble down to the middle of your chest, dabble across to the front of the left shoulder, and dabble across to the front of the right shoulder]. Forms the sign of a cross over body. "Peace to this house and all who dwell within it." [Sprinkle water in room; show no fear; feel the words you say].

WHITE LIGHT PROTECTION PRAYER
I call upon the white light of protection to come forth from the golden orb above my head, covering my entire body from the top of my head to the bottom of my feet, through each chakra extending through my entire aura. This white light surrounds, protects, heals and guides me, going within to further protect, cleanse, purify and heal, totally permeating my entire being. I ask that any and all negative, sickly, jealous, evil, or mean energies, entities, spirits, guides, or vibrations that have attached themselves to me or are within my presence be sent back to their source, never to return to seek me out. I ask this blessing with neither love nor hate, but for sake of the greatest good. In the name of the almighty, I thank you.

Messages

It Makes No Difference To Me If You Do Not Believe … Science Cannot Explain Everything.

Quoted by
Kelly Renee Schutz

Illustration – Photo Taken by Kelly Renee Schutz

Just Because You Can't See Me Doesn't Mean I'm Not Here.

Illustration – Photo Taken by Kelly Renee Schutz

When I Was Young, I Had Always Wanted To See A Ghost, Now I Can't Seem To Get Rid Of Them.

*Quoted by
Kelly Renee Schutz*

Art Illustration by George Patsouras

Some ghosts want attention, others simply want you to pay attention.

Experienced by
Kelly Renee Schutz

Art Illustration by Brandy Woods

I Touch Your Things. I Sit In Your Chair. I Lie On Your Bed. You Can't See Me – But I Can See You.

Art Illustration by Magdalena Adic

When I Look Into Your Eyes, I See Your Soul. When I Experience A Ghostly Encounter, I Feel Its Soul.

Quoted by
Kelly Renee Schutz

Photo Taken by Kelly Renee Schutz

Laws of Naturalism – "the idea or belief that only natural laws and forces operate in the physical world." Oxford English Dictionary, (2016)

Art Illustration by Brandy Woods
Can Someone Explain To Me If These Orbs Are Natural?

Chapter 1
Behind the Curtain

Illustration by Brandy Woods

Chapter 1
Behind the Curtain

<u>PHENOMENA</u>

You feel something is residing behind a closed curtain. You hear sounds of laughter coming from the kitchen. You smell something decomposing in a room and become overwhelmed with illness. A music box starts to play without it being touched. A jar containing baby teeth jumps out in front of you falling over on a table. A curtain located on the second level of the house catches on fire but extinguishes itself. A tornado wind hits the house causing damage but not enough to condemn it. Do I believe my former grandparent's home was haunted and protected by "something" who didn't like house guests? Yes. Prior to my grandparents taking ownership of this home, it was reported that a previous owner, a woman, was burned to death by a fire in a porch adjacent to the kitchen. It is believed this woman was not ready to leave this home and was angry with those being there. My grandparents were strong Catholic believers whose faith did not engage in paranormal occurrences post-death. In fact, in a brief discussion with my grandmother once, I recall asking her if she ever thought her house was haunted. To which ... she just giggled and told me it wasn't.

TRAGIC INCIDENTS

When "someone" appears to hang around a specific location after their death has occurred, it seems as though we want to believe that this "someone" is or was a former resident. Theories suggest people who pass away suddenly from tragic incidents such as murder, violent crime, suicide, tragic accident, or unexpected death (overdose, illness) may not know their soul has moved out of their physical body and continue to participate in life as if they never left it. Others, who have passed on may be: (1) unwilling or unable to crossover to an astral plane, (2) could be watching over their loved ones or property, or in some cases, (3) are lost or stuck on earth not knowing how to depart from it.

DEFINITIONS

Apparition or entity – a spirit that has a soul, consciousness, or mind, surviving the death of its body capable of interacting with the living (may be seen, heard, felt, or smelled). **Astral plane** - a world believed to exist above our physical world. **Attack** – a feeling of weakness, low energy, dizzy, sick stomach, ill, or overcome by strong or rotting smells, such as deceased animals or strong scents. **Clairaudience** - an auditory form of ESP paranormal information that is received outside the range of normal perception through hearing voices, whispers, and auditory impressions.

Coincidence – concurrence of events or circumstances without apparent causal connection. **False awakening** - an event where the person thinks they are awake but they are really dreaming. **Sensitive** - the ability to perceive information through extrasensory perception (ESP). **Subjective apparition** - a hallucination of apparitions or other phenomena created in our minds. **Telekinesis** – ability to control one's physical environment without using physical manipulation or force. **Trigger** – activating feelings experienced in the past. **Trigger Object** – a person or object used to cause or elicit reactions from unseen energies [ghosts].

THE ENCOUNTERS

OVERLY SENSITIVE. My former grandparent's home was built in 1890. They took possession of it around 1955 or 1956. This would be their second home in the same town. Between the ages of 9 and 17, I would have days when I would need to stay at their home alone while they were out running errands or on vacation. Their home was known as a safe place to go for my siblings and myself, a place where we stayed when babysat, ill, spent time with them, or waited for our mother to pick us up after school.

During my visits at this home, I would feel anxious or nervous being alone. My excuse then was because it was an unfamiliar environment, it caused me to experience anxiety.

To combat my anxiety of being there alone, I would wander the first main floor rooms, watch television, sing or talk out loud, or try to nap to pass the time away. On some occasions, I would sense unexplained moments of feeling anxious often escalating into panic attacks. Panic attacks where I would start to physically perspire. As I aged, I thought my **sensitivities** to being there would lessen. However, my anxiousness would appear to intensify leading to more sweating or stomach aches.

QUESTIONS AND THOUGHTS

Unfamiliar homes, buildings, and spaces, regardless of age, seem to captivate overactive imaginations making most anxious people feel threatened by its environment. Was I experiencing anxiety or a **subjective apparition** in this home? Why was I unable to grow out of my feeling nervous being in this house alone at an older age?

THE KITCHEN LAUGHTER. All houses – old or new - have their noises and construction settling quirks. Built in 1890, few renovations were made to this home with most updates being made to the outside exterior. This home appeared to have no hidden secrets. In the basement lie a dirt floor (unfinished) and would be visited often by my grandfather who cleaned his catch of the day (fish) in a sink down there. A wooden floor (2nd story floor) would squeak when stepped on, typical of old plank floors.

One day, while I was in the house alone, I decided to take a nap to combat my feeling anxious. A few hours into my nap, I would awaken to hear loud noises, mumble, and laughter coming from the kitchen. Thinking I must have been out of it to not hear my grandparents return from their errands, I got up and in a sleepy daze, proceeded to wander to the kitchen.

As I approached the doorway leading into the kitchen, the loud talking and laughter would suddenly stop. Looking into an empty kitchen, my eyes would gaze intently at the table ... and then ... look to the door leading down into the basement ... and then ... look out the window. I saw no human existence. Confused and with my heart racing, I went back to the couch to finish my nap while breaking out in a nervous sweat.

QUESTIONS AND THOUGHTS

The sounds of laughter and noises awakened me from my nap. Did I just sense a moment being **clairaudient** yet finding no one in the kitchen? Or, did I experience a **false awakening**? Those who pass tragically at a location (the kitchen) may return to it as the setting may be of most comfort to them. The mumbling, laughter, and noise created from the kitchen was loud enough to wake me up. Not finding anyone in the kitchen (dead silent) brought about a sweating and suspicious reaction from me.

AFTER THE INCIDENT. After this kitchen laughter incident occurred, I would find myself on "alone days" either sitting in their bathroom with the doors closed (they had two doors) or in their sun porch (cold or hot weather), with the door leading inside to the house locked (by me). In absolute emergencies, I would go inside to use the restroom or telephone. When asked why I would sit in the sun porch and not go inside, I would make excuses or simply say something to effect that it was unnerving being inside the house. Of course, the reaction back to me was, "that's crazy, what's wrong with you" ... "there's nothing in the house to be afraid of." In my mind though, "yes, there was."

My feelings of uneasiness continued to escalate every time I stayed there alone. I thought I could overcome these feelings as I grew older. No. As I briefly did before, I would ask my grandmother if she thought her house was haunted. To which I would get another stunned reaction, "that's nonsense." I was now convinced that my fear being in that house alone was nothing more than my imagination getting the best of me. When I found myself having moments of anxiety, I would turn the volume up on the television, turn all the lights on, sing loudly, talk non-stop, keep the inside door from the house to the sun porch open, sit alone in the bathroom with both doors closed, and sometimes, would leave the house and sit outside on the steps. Paranoid? I could never overcome this feeling.

CLOSED CURTAIN. Perhaps what frightened me the most was the closed curtain at the top of the stairs that led up to the second floor. With its heavy, dark material used to keep the cold and heat air drafts behind it, I would suffer from anxiety with every step I took until I reached the top before grabbing it and pulling it open. Add to this heart stopping moment, the musky scent the curtain gave off because it hung so long without being washed. Now, we have a smell sensation engaging with fear.

GRANDMOTHER PASSES. Years began to pass and my visits to my grandparent's home lessened. Eventually, I would grieve the loss of my grandmother (nearly 90 years old), who suffered from a massive stroke in that home while sitting in her chair watching her favorite TV daytime show, *General Hospital*. She passed away in the hospital. My grandfather would remain in that house until a few years later but would grow lonely. He would eventually be moved into a nursing home. His age when he moved to the nursing home was 96 years old. His age when he passed was 103 years old. He died of natural causes.

THE VISIT. I must have been around the age of 35 (my grandfather was still living in the nursing home) when we (children) were allowed inside the house to look around at its current state of condition. I recall my nervousness entering the home (alone) but felt more confident as an adult than as a child-teen being there.

As I walked through the front door (alone), the feelings I had once felt as a child-teen began to resurface in my mind with every step I took. The mission of my visit that day was to go upstairs and view what had been left in boxes. I didn't spend much time looking around inside the house. I felt like I was being watched no matter where I stood. As I approached the stairs, I looked up toward the closed curtain. Taking a deep breath, I made my way up each step feeling more uptight as I reached the top. The emotions I had felt as a child-teen were **triggered** by my memories being there alone. I recall telling myself that I had nothing to fear. That fell on deaf ears and mind.

TOP OF STAIRS. As I grabbed the curtain and pushed it aside, it would take me a few minutes to calm my nerves in order to acclimate to the conditions around me. The smell of the musky curtain was as strong as ever with dust falling off it. My first and only stop would be the pink bedroom to view a few boxes of memorabilia.

As I walked into the pink room, the air felt light but had a hint of an old aged wood scent. The original bed I had slept on as a child (one or two times) remained in the room. The room appeared smaller than I had once remembered. Sitting on the edge of the bed, I grabbed my first box to look at memorabilia. *What I didn't know at the time was that something was in that room watching my every move.*

ATTACKED. As I began to glance at each item in the box, it was no more than ten minutes when I began feeling sick to my stomach. Symptoms that came on suddenly were a mild headache, feeling dizzy, fuzzy thinking (like my head was in a drum), and stomach pains. These symptoms were puzzling to me feeling because I had felt fine entering the home. I was now experiencing illness. It was also at this point that the room conditions changed (from light air to heavy air). My breathing began to labor. I reminded myself that there was nothing to fear thinking I was triggering myself to have a panic attack.

I was probably in that room no more than fifteen minutes total when I felt the air getting heavier and an intense smell of something rotten or decomposing (deceased animal) drifting around me. I looked toward the wall thinking a mouse may have died in it. I noticed the burnt curtain. It is believed a lightning strike hitting the house may have caused this. I got up from the bed and attempted to locate the rotten smell. Having a sensitive nose, I would have noticed this rotting dead smell immediately upon my entrance into the room. In fact, the rotting dead smell continued to **intensify** the longer I stayed in the room. Not finding the source, I sat back down and continued to look at memorabilia. It would not be long until I would find myself putting my hands over my nose to not breathe in the horrid smell. Finally, there came a point where I could not stand it anymore and left quickly running down the stairs and out of the house.

WHAT JUST HAPPENED TO ME? You may ask if I could have been experiencing a chemical or toxic smell that went unnoticed until I became adjusted to the environment. I'm not sure. I know sitting houses have their smells, especially 100-year old houses. Dead mice smell badly but would have been noticed upon my entrance into the room. Could my headache and dizziness been caused by unseen molds or toxins? I didn't get the impression there was a mold problem in the house. I am convinced I was **attacked** by something negative who just wanted me out of that house. Feeling good when I went into it and leaving feeling very ill makes me wonder about what was lurking from behind the curtain.

QUESTIONS – THOUGHTS - AFTERMATH

Do I believe I was the target of something negative in that house? Yes. Do I believe it was the former owner (woman) who died in the porch fire? Yes. The house was built around 1898. It still stands as of this writing (modified). Two owners have been in possession of it since my grandparent's death. The house is one of the few remaining in this town at this age. Did others in my family experience unexplained uneasiness in this house? Yes. At what age did others in my family notice? Around the ages of 4 to 8. Did my mother who lived in that house as a teen for a short period of time ever notice anything? No.

When the house was sold at auction in 1995, a young man purchased it on a contract for deed (just short of $30,000). His intent was to remodel the first and second levels. While deconstructing wall or rafter upstairs, a 50-cent piece fell out of it. It dated back to the late 1800's. The value of this coin was around $50.00. In his efforts to remodel, he ran out of money and moved. A family with young children purchased the home thereafter. No idea if they had ever experienced anything negative in the house.

OTHER ENCOUNTERS IN HOME

THE ESTATE PICKING. The next time I would enter my grandparent's home would be during an estate picking with my family. As a side note, I have always been apprehensive about acquiring items from auctions or estates due to entity (paranormal) attachments to objects.

During the estate picking, I did not go upstairs to the pink room. While item picking, two unexplained incidents occurred with one happening to my younger sister, who is also sensitive, and the other incident, to me. To be discussed after you read "definitions."

DEFINITIONS

Agent – a living person who is the focus of poltergeist activity. **Poltergeist** – non-human entity (noisy ghost) usually more malicious or destructive than ghosts or deceased human beings. May involve thumping, banging, levitation or movement of objects, stone throwing, and starting fires. **Intuition** – perceptive insight ("gut feeling"). **Synchronicity** – numerous unrelated variables joining to create a common event or coincidence.

THE MUSIC BOX. During the estate picking, two incidents occurred that involved a **synchronization** of a music box and teeth jar (story follows). A music box was lying on my grandparent's bed. How it got placed onto the bed remains unknown. Tables had been set up in the livingroom displaying our grandparent's possessions for viewing. My sister recalled she was looking at stuff on a table when she overheard a music box playing. She followed the sound to an adjacent room on the first floor which led her into our grandparent's bedroom. The music box (playing) intrigued her enough to pick it up to inspect it. The pin, which is typically pulled out after winding to make the music box play, remained in a locked position (it should not have played). Startled by this observation, she put it down onto the bed and came and told me about it while I was looking at items on tables.

As I went into the bedroom to investigate, the music box had stopped playing.

THE TEETH JAR. Thinking my sister was imagining things with that music box turned my attention to a table in front of me that had a jar with a mix of several baby teeth in it. It just so happens my grandparents saved our baby teeth they had pulled (my siblings and cousins) displaying them in a jar they placed in their cupboard.

Side Note: My grandfather prided himself in his teeth pulling methods such as using a string attached to a door, a wrench the size of a fist, and all other types of tooth extraction methods. You would think the fear of him using those methods alone would make the tooth fall out on its own.

I recall no one touching anything on any of the tables during the viewing session. I also remember the room was still with no chaotic movement or vibration causing items to topple over on their own. In fact, all items on the tables sat secured in their positions. I was puzzled when I spotted a jar half full of baby teeth. What I shouldn't have done was make a snide comment about it … "why would anyone collect and store teeth in a jar?" As others were distracted looking elsewhere, it was at the point of my comment that jar "jumped" toward me falling on top of other items.

Everyone heard something fall and looked in my direction. I explained I had nothing do with the jar falling but told them it jumped at me on its own. They looked at me with blank stares and in disbelief.

QUESTIONS / THOUGHTS

Could these moments have been a **synchronization** of paranormal activity? The music box and the teeth jar? Was there an entity present? Or were these moments just pure coincidence? How many coincidences must occur before **intuition** is tossed to the wind? Music boxes don't play in a shut off mode positions, or do they? Teeth jars do not jump at someone when solidly positioned on a table, or do they? As I look back on these situations, it is apparent to me that something was trying to get our attention. I do not believe it was the spirit of my grandmother. My grandfather was still alive and in the nursing home.

SIDE NOTE. When the teeth jar jumped at me, I did make a comment to all in the room that no more remarks should be made about our grandparent's possessions. A belief I have about the afterlife is that they can still hear us. To this day, I also do not make fun of objects picked at auctions, estate sales, or garage sales. I have since experienced other "jumping objects" in my husband's presence with no conclusive explanation other than most incidents seem to occur during a new or full moon phase.

CURTAIN FIRE. Is it possible for ghosts to protect the homes in which they had once lived or feel comfortable in? I speculate the answer to this question might be, "maybe." Although I cannot offer evidence or proof of my opinion, there have been some very interesting weather events that should have caused damage to my grandparent's house to the point of its full destruction.

LIGHTNING STRIKE. My grandparent's home was hit by a lightning strike shortly after my grandfather was moved into a nursing home. The lightning strike caused the curtain on the second floor (pink room) to start on fire. This is the same room I felt I was attacked in. Although this curtain should have blazed into flames, it was as if something had patted it out leaving singed edges. Coincidence? Maybe. Could it be possible that the material it was made was flame retardant? Doubtful. Recall, this house had a fire in the kitchen causing the death of a woman years before my grandparent's took possession of it. Could the curtain fire been put out by "something" wanting to protect its comfortable home? I say anything is possible.

TORNADO. It was within a year or two after the curtain fire incident when a F4 tornado would hit the town (grandfather still in nursing home) causing widespread damage to many homes. Many of the homes near and next to my grandparent's house had to be torn down.

Damage to my grandparent's home included all windows being broken, a board pierced through the wall from the outside into the kitchen, police radio found in the middle of the dining room floor along with a bunch of money (paper, not coins) next to it.

Was destruction of the home spared by the unpredictable wind currents of the storm? Or, was there something in the home that offered its assistance in protecting it? These questions may never get answered. I have always been fascinated by the bizarre effects of weather. Hearing a piece of straw pierced a tree (right through its trunk) ... almost like threading a needle. Vehicles ending up in other people's garages perfectly parked and untouched. Houses lifted from their foundation and found in the backyards on other people's properties. It is no wonder that something as odd as finding a police radio along with money in the middle of the dining room floor ... should not be as surprising as it sounds.

Chapter 2
Ouija Board – "Butter Damn'it"

Illustration by Brandy Woods

Chapter 2
Ouija Board – "Butter Damn'it"

PHENOMENA

Unexplained events in a Minnesota home such as cupboard doors opening, water faucets turning on and off by themselves, and lights flickering to voice commands would cause enough alarm for two high school teachers and two seniors to use a Ouija board to attempt contact with "something" they felt resided in the home. As contact is made through the Ouija board, the spirit reprimands all of them for not putting butter on the popcorn while providing specific information about a dying young girl who lived in New York.

WORD OF WARNING – USE OF OUIJA BOARDS

"Ouija" comes from the French (oui) and German (ja) words meaning "yes." The game board is pre-printed with letters and numbers on it in which a planchette (marker) is placed on top (lightly touched with fingers) in order to communicate with spirits. Once contact is made, the marker moves to spell out letters and numbers aiding in answering questions. As reported by many, the board can be bad luck to play with if unprotected. Ouija boards can bring or summon negative or demonic spirits other than those sought after into our world.

In some cases, those who have used the board have experienced a string of negative events or bad luck. Even if these incidents are merely coincidental, it is difficult to rid an area of an evil spirit that has been summoned through a Ouija board.

According to the Free Dictionary (2016), an **evil spirit** is described as having "a shape-shifting non-human spirit that usually appears after being summoned, either by use of a Ouija board or through satanic worship." The evil spirit can appear as a monster or may disguise itself to be friendly. Its intent is dangerous and seeks to harm or cause destruction. Some have reported trying to rid or destroy the board by returning it to where it was purchased or found, burying it, throwing it into a river, or burning it. In some cases, after getting rid of the board, the experiences continue.

DEFINITIONS

Anomaly – irregular or unusual event that does not follow a standard rule or law or that cannot be explained by currently accepted scientific theories. **Automatism** – unconscious or involuntary muscular movement caused by spirits. **Automatic Writing** – method used to obtain information from disembodied spirits where the spirit takes control over the individuals causing them to translate unconscious information on paper without being aware of its contents. **Channeling** – form of spirit communication where a spirit will pass information directly to a channeler who will then relay the information to its listener(s). **Contact Session** – period in which investigators attempt to establish communication with an entity. **Intelligent Haunting** – interaction with a spirit on the physical plane where there is oral (words) or visual communication (object movement).

THE ENCOUNTER

While I was not there or witnessed the contact made through this Ouija board session, the write-up about it was in our high school newspaper (year 1977-1978). The article was so compelling that it convinced me enough to never forget about it. As of this writing, one of the teachers involved in this session, is currently the superintendent of the High School. I was in my sophomore year (10th grade) during this time and was a contributor for the newspaper.

The individuals involved in this encounter were two of my high school teachers and two senior students. Although I cannot speak to their honesty, they all appeared to have good reputations and credibility. The teachers (married) were having an ongoing issue in their house with odd occurrences. The two seniors, who used a Ouija board regularly for fun, reached out to help the teachers. It should be noted that back in the day, we did not have access to seek out other sources, such as psychics.

As a student in high school in the mid 1970's, it was unheard of then to be able to call up a psychic on the phone to inquire about a mischievous ghost. In fact, back in the day, psychics were known as scammers and did not hold the respect many of them do in this day. The only means to contact an entity was by use of a Ouija board (which had, at this time, no harmful reputation and was noted as a toy for fun).

MAKING CONTACT. It was one weekend evening when the four gathered together at the teachers' home to attempt to contact the resident ghost. It was agreed by all to set up the Ouija board in the livingroom. They sat in the dark with only lit candles to see what messages they might receive from it.

As each person took turns asking basic questions (for example, "who are you" ... "where did you come from" ... "what messages do you need to tell us") ... they received no response. An hour or two had gone by and just as they were about to give up playing with the board, one of the high school seniors felt her hands involuntarily moving (**automatism**) over letters spelling out words. Feeling they had made **contact** with something, they were intrigued and continued playing **channeling** the spirit.

At some point, the unknown entity believed to be their resident ghost, asked for popcorn with butter on it. Playing along, one of the seniors went to the kitchen to make some. While in the kitchen, it was discovered there was no butter available. The person returned to the group sharing the popcorn. Soon after, the upset ghost spelled out onto the Ouija board, "butter, damn'it!"

Astonished by what just happened, the group began probing for answers to their questions with what appeared to be with an **intelligent** ghost. What came next as a response from the entity would offer confusion to this story. The ghost spelled out a name of a five-year old girl who was dying in New York. This entity also spelled out her address. What makes this story more interesting is that this little girl lived approximately 1200 miles away from the state in which this was session was being conducted in. The ghost stated to the group that it was on a mission to help the little girl because she was dying. Curious, the teachers wrote to the address to inquire. They received a response back in return from the mother of this little girl asking how they knew of her address and affirmed that they did have a daughter dying of an illness.

QUESTIONS AND THOUGHTS

Is it possible for a ghost to taste what a person eats? I am going to lean in the direction of, "maybe." After all, a ghost doesn't have taste buds ... right? Is it possible for people OR ghosts to experience what is called **clairgustince?**

According to Stambaugh (2013), **clairgustince** is the "ability to perceive or experience taste without putting anything in the mouth." I have personally experienced readings with psychics over the phone where they could tell me what I had been eating. How is this ability to taste possible? If this is possible, then, is it likely that ghosts are capable of spiritual interaction with us or even bodily possession?

LET'S THINK ABOUT THIS STORY

There are a few niches in this story that confuse me. First, why would a nice ghost be upset that butter wasn't added to the popcorn? Second, why would a ghost be haunting someone's home continuously only to inform them that their mission was to comfort a dying young girl who lived 1200 miles away? Even though the address and child's story appeared to be coincidentally accurate, do you think that perhaps their visit was not by a "nice" ghost, but rather, by an "evil" spirit disguising itself to be a caring, nice ghost? When an evil spirit wants to cause issues or illness, its main mission is to get close to someone willing to let their guard down so it can take trick the person. One way of doing this is to pretend it is something it is not.

Is it possible the entity the teachers were initially experiencing in their home was that of a resident ghost? After playing with the Ouija board, is it possible they brought something else into their home? An odd coincidence, the teachers divorced a few years later.

Chapter 3
"Bring It On" – Rubber Ducky

Illustration by Brandy Woods

Litchfield Plantation, Pawleys Island, South Carolina

Chapter 3
"Bring It On" – Rubber Ducky

<u>PHENOMENA</u>

You receive a warning from the check-in host, "you do realize there are no refunds if you decide to leave?" You hear footsteps walking into your villa, but no one is there. Your door to your bedroom appears stuck and won't open causing panic between you and your husband. You hear noises in your bathroom all night with no cause or movement of any object. Your television sparks turning itself off while you are lying in bed. A rubber ducky, positioned on a hot tub, is moved across the room to a ledge, situated in a locked room. You hear rustling noises outside in a dense forest situated next to a stream, but it is so dark you can't see anything. Staying in a haunted villa on the Litchfield Plantation, near Myrtle Beach, South Carolina taught us one very important lesson - never taunt a ghost.

<u>WHAT NOT TO SAY TO A GHOST</u>

What you should never say to a ghost is "BRING IT ON!" A phrase and reminder to my husband to think twice before mocking or shouting his disbelief that ghosts do not exist. Of strong Catholic faith, my husband believes strongly in angels but will on occasion, admit to having his doubts about the non-existence of ghosts. As a result, the ghosts that like to hang around me like to taunt him. My general rule of thumb is to be respectful and nice to the "afterlife."

DEFINITIONS

Afterlife – often referred to as "life after death." Most ghost hunters avoid using specific religious terms such as "heaven" when discussing ghosts, hauntings, and the afterlife. **Amulet** – an object that is thought to bring good luck or have the power to protect from ghosts or spirits warding off evil. **Earthbound** – a ghost or spirit unable to cross over to the other side at the time of death and is therefore stuck on earth. **Hoax** – a preplanned series of events to give the impression that something paranormal has been occurring in any given place. **Intelligent Haunting** – interaction on the physical plane involving either verbal (words) or physical movement of objects. **Poltergeist** – a noisy ghost, also known for its presence of sounds such as footsteps, tapping on walls, disappearance of items, foul odors, cold spots, etc. **Skeptic** – to question what others may perceive as real.

HISTORY OF LITCHFIELD PLANTATION

The information provided below is credited to all the writers and researchers who extensively pieced together an organized biography about the history of Litchfield Plantation.

Litchfield Plantation is located on the Waccamaw River and is accessible from Kings River Rd on Pawleys Island, South Carolina. The original plantation land was located north of Waverly Creek and stretched from the Waccamaw River all the way to the Atlantic Ocean including much of what is called Litchfield Beach.

The plantation's earliest date of existence was around 1710 and comprised 3 separate land grants given to Thomas Hepworth by King George II. The original three land grants were 500, 420, and 500 acres given in 1710, 1711 and 1712. The plantation was named Litchfield by Peter Simon with the first reported statement of its existence being in his last will in testament. Peter Simon built the original plantation house in 1740 (still stands as of this writing) now operating as a wedding and event center. The plantation in the mid 1700's grew more than 100 million pounds of Carolina Gold rice, which required the help of about 150 slaves. The entire property hosts hundreds of Regal oak trees over the 600 acres.[1,2,3]

SIMON. On November 10, 1794, Peter Simon died and the property was divided between his 2 sons. John Simon, one of his sons, inherited Litchfield, a southern parcel that was narrow stretching from the river all the way to the sea shore. Not long after John Simon inherited the property, he sold his portion of Litchfield Plantation to the Tucker family who became the most well-known owners. The Tucker family owned the plantation from 1796 until 1897, with three generations of Tuckers calling the plantation home and ending with the ownership of Dr. Henry Tucker.[1,2,3]

TUCKER. The Tucker family came to South Carolina from Bermuda. Daniel Tucker was a politician and had three sons. The eldest son was John Tucker who eventually inherited the plantation and perfected methods for growing rice. By 1850, Litchfield Plantation was producing over one million pounds of rice each year.[1,2,3]

Upon the death of John Tucker, the property passed to his son Dr. Henry Massingberd Tucker. Dr. Tucker served as a volunteer with the Confederate Army for four years during the Civil War. He was also a staunch Episcopalian and when a new church was built he had the old All Saints Church dismantled and moved to his property.[1,2,3]

It is rumored Dr. Tucker's ghost still visits the property regularly. The ghost of Dr. Tucker has been seen at the main house in the Blue Room, which was his bedroom, and on the back staircase that he used late at night when returning home from house calls. Dr. Tucker was also a sportsman and won many tournaments at the Georgetown Rifle Club.[1,2,3]

Very little information is recorded on the history of slaves at Litchfield Plantation, although it is established by many sources that slaves were used to work the plantation and other plantations in the area. One of the most distinguishing characteristics of Litchfield Plantation is the existence of a cemetery used by slaves of Litchfield Plantation and their descendants. According to an archaeological investigation performed by Brockington and Associates in 1989, the cemetery holds about 150 possible graves. Only 2 of those graves are marked with dates 1888, and 1920.[1,2,3]

Louis Claude Lachicotte, part of Breslauer, Lachicotte and Company, bought Litchfield Plantation from Dr. Tucker in 1897 and started South Carolinas first canning factory that packed vegetables and seafood at the plantation. The Lachicottes sold the property 14 years later in 1911 to Joshua John Ward of Brookgreen and Arthur Herbert Lachicotte of Waverly and they held the property until 1926.[1,2,3]

Dr. Henry Norris purchased Litchfield Plantation in 1926 and restored much of the original plantation house. He repaired the home and added a wing on both sides of it.

Dr. Norris became a generous benefactor to the Waccamaw community. During the time he owned the property he landscaped and developed the grounds. He also built the wrought iron gates and brick gateway at the entrance of the property.[1,2,3]

Later the Parker family and J.P. Booth continued and extended Norris vision by landscaping the old brick street to the north of the house. Also during this time, the Azaleas were added to line the avenue of oaks and the reflection pool was added to the front lawn of the main house.[1,2,3]

Litchfield Plantation's modern history began in 1969 when the Plantation was sold to Litchfield Plantation Company and development began to create an upscale, gated neighborhood.[1]

AS OF JANUARY 2016. The original plantation mansion, as of this date, is used as a Country Inn, and the original site of the stables is now occupied by The Carriage House Club, a private dining club.[1]

CHRONOLOGICAL LIST OF OWNERS[2]

Peter Simon, circa 1794
John Simon, circa 1794 (acquired upon death of
    Peter Simon; sold to Daniel Tucker prior to 1796)
Daniel Tucker, circa 1794-1797
John Hyrne Tucker, 1797-1859
Dr. Henry Massingberd Tucker, 1859-1897
Breslauer, Lachicotte and Company, 1897-1901
Louis Claude Lachicotte, 1901-1904
Col. Ralph Nesbit, 1904-1911
Joshua John Ward and Arthur Herbert Lachicotte,
    1911-1926
Dr. Henry Norris, 1926-1942

Harry Edmond Parker, J. Philip Booth and Thornwell
 Hay Parker, 1942-1957
James B. Moore, E. Craig Wall, William N. Miller, Jr.,
 Howard Hinman, Jr., 1957-1966
Louise Price Parsons, 1966-1969
Litchfield Plantation Company – 1969-2013
John Miller – acquired June 2013-present[3]

OTHER HAUNTINGS. The description of the ghostly visits made by Dr. Tucker in the plantation house have been reported several times but of course have not been factually verified.

Other reports suggest back when the gates were made of wood and not of iron, the kind Dr. Tucker would come back home after visiting a patient or a leisurely horse ride and would ring the bell outside the gates of Litchfield. This would signal a gatekeeper who lived nearby to let Dr. Tucker into the property.

During times when the gatekeeper would slip away, Dr. Tucker would ring the bell furiously getting no answer. He would then tie his horse to the fence and climb over to walk to the house where, if it was late in the evening, he would use a private staircase to avoid disturbing his family.

STAIRS. Long after the doctor's death, people claimed to see him wearing a uniform while sitting on the stairs or walking up to his room. Some people would report hearing a horse trotting up the lane towards the main house. Others would hear the clanging of the bell at any hour of the night as though the doctor was trying to get the gatekeeper's attention. It was this sound that caused one owner to remove the bell entirely to prevent the doctor from disturbing his and others sleep.

MONA. Mona is reported to be another ghost haunting the property. Mona, age 16, one of the caretaker's daughters, either drowned or died on the property. She is seen wearing a blue or pink dress. She, and possible haunts by former slaves, have occurred in various locations on the property.

OUR ENCOUNTERS

The landscape of Litchfield Plantation has changed significantly since our visit there in 2003. Driving through the gate, you drove slowly down a 2-lane road, swamp on one side with old regal oak trees with hanging moss from their limbs on the other. The atmosphere gave you a sense that you were being watched as you made your way to the plantation house. Our being unnerved by the grand driveway entrance, we anxiously anticipated the excitement of encountering a ghostly adventure.

CHECK-IN. I recall our check-in as if it happened yesterday. A woman, in her mid-50's, and dressed very professionally, was sitting at a desk as we walked in. My recollection was that she told us very few guests were allowed to stay in the plantation home due to its age. Therefore, we were assigned to stay in a 4-bedroom villa on the property. Because we were drawn to this property due to its known ghostly activity in the plantation house, this news brought sheer disappointment and speculation. She assured us that we would be in the 4-bedroom villa by ourselves. Knowing what I know now, I wish she would have booked a few other villa guests with us that evening. She finalized our booking by saying, "you are aware that this property is haunted" ... to which I replied, "yes, but if we are not in the plantation house, I doubt we will experience anything." Her comment was, "don't be so sure about that." The property was huge and the roads to find our villa were confusing. I grumbled all the way to our villa. Once we got there, we attempted to make the best of our situation.

We found our villa and parked near the front of it. I recall feeling disappointed as I looked at its outward appearance lacking in appeal. It was at this point that we began to wonder if the advertising for this property (as being haunted) was nothing more than a **hoax** to get us there. Time of arrival to our villa was around 6:00 PM.

As we got out of the car, we both walked cautiously toward the villa. Located in a heavily wooded area, my husband, knowing how upset I was that we would not be staying in the plantation house, decided to blurt out as we walked through the front door …**"BRING IT ON, GHOSTS."**

This comment would turn his being **skeptic** into his "famous last words." It was as if the ghosts were sitting in the villa waiting for our arrival making it a point to stick around to pester us all evening. My husband always carried a rosary [**amulet**] in his pocket for protection.

ENTRANCE. As we walked into the villa, we proceeded down a short foyer observing a modern kitchen to our right and stairs to the left. We continued to roam past a common area livingroom, a main area for all guests staying in this villa, to get to our bedroom. I recall making a comment that we were right next to the livingroom and that if anyone else was booked there, we would get no sleep due to their noise. Well, no one else was booked there that evening but we still didn't get much sleep.

BEDROOM. Being tired from our trip, as I opened the door to our villa bedroom, its appearance inside made me feel immediately comfortable and at ease. What a beautiful room. For just a minute, it took away all the uneasy feelings about the property being haunted and put me in a state of ahhhh. I proceeded to rummage through our bags finding an outfit to get ready for our night out.

HUSBAND DISAPPEARS / FOOTSTEPS. As we were getting ready to go out for supper, my husband decided to roam the villa to check out its internal arrangement of rooms. Shortly after his disappearance, I heard the front door open along with footsteps. I thought to myself that another couple must have been booked with us for the evening. I walked out of the room to greet our mystery guests only to discover after saying "HELLO," that no one answered and of course, no one was there.

"ANYONE HERE?" No response. I then became bewildered and yelled for my husband who was upstairs in a back area. I said to him, "did you just open the front door and walk down the foyer entrance?" As I said this, I was looking at him at the top of the stairs. "No, I have been up here the entire time." He was standing on carpet. I told him I heard someone open the door and come in. I told him to come down. Being somewhat confused, I made him look outside to determine if anyone was parked next to us, made him recreate the front door opening and footsteps, and concluded that I was "hearing things." We left to go to a restaurant.

DOOR WON'T OPEN. As we sat at the restaurant, the door and foyer moment continued to replay in my mind. I recall arriving back to the property in pitch dark and not wanting to go back inside the villa. The entire property started to feel creepy and was getting the best of me. My husband asked me if I wanted to stay somewhere else for the evening, to which I said, "I would like to but we came here for me to experience a ghost encounter, so, we need to stay." As we walked back into the villa (now in creepy dark conditions), I told him to NOT say or taunt what might be waiting inside for us. Once inside, we went to our room.

I cannot recall why my husband needed to leave for a minute but on his way out of the room, I made him shut the door taking the keys with him. I proceeded to sit on the bed until his arrival back. On his arrival back, he couldn't get his key to open the door. Thinking he must have lost his mind because we had no problem opening the door upon our arrival, I went over to the door and tried to open it from the inside. I couldn't get it open either. We struggled from his side and mine. And then, suddenly and without additional effort, it released itself and opened on its own. This was very strange. My anxiety now turns into fear.

DARK PORCH – RUBBER DUCKY. Trying to shake that moment off, we decided to go out to the sun porch (attached to our room located behind the building). It was pitch dark outside and we couldn't see anything beyond the sun porch. We heard noises rustling in the trees and a water stream (creek) flowing but saw nothing. Talk about freaking a person out. The porch had a hot tub. Neither of us felt like using it. What we did notice was a yellow rubber ducky sitting on the ledge of the hot tub. I do recall both of us commenting about it. Making sure the sun porch door leading to the outside was latched, we went back inside and locked the door from our room leading into it. As we were in bed, we began to talk about how paranoid I felt being there. My husband tried to assure me that nothing was there. But ... he was WRONG.

LYING IN BED. At this point, I didn't feel very well. I lied in bed suffering from head congestion. My husband turned on the television. I asked him to keep the volume low because I had a headache. I rolled over to my side looking toward the middle of the room. It was probably no more than 15 minutes later when he said, "what the hell" (television had shut off abruptly throwing sparks at us). He asked me if I shut the television off, to which I replied, "I have no idea where the remote is." He told me that sparks just flew out of the TV at him and that it turned off by itself.

It was at this point when I made him apologize to whatever he taunted because I knew that we were not alone in that room. Thinking his apology would calm the environment down, we no sooner than turned the television back on when another surprise awaited us.

SIDE NOTE - TV SPARKS. You are probably thinking ... "well, my television sparks all the time when I shut it off" (giving a loud snap and flash). This is not what we experienced. This would not be the only time we would experience what appeared to be paranormal associated sparks shooting out of something electrical. The television may have shut off but was wired to electricity. I have seen the same thing happen to hand held cameras and video camcorders. In these cases, the sparks would turn batteries dead and the equipment would immediately malfunction. We have even awoken to our TV turning on by itself (where our remote was unreachable).

NOISES IN BATHROOM. Soon after the sparks episode, apparently, my husband wasn't convinced enough that we were in the company of "something." He turned the TV back on and within minutes, we began hearing noises coming from our bathroom. The noises sounded like someone was taking my make-up eyeliner pencil and dropping it onto the floor giving off the sound that it was rolling. This happened over and over and over. I made my husband go into the bathroom to investigate the noises and to look at the shower drain in case some animal got into the room. Nothing. My make-up was sitting right where I had left it. Nothing had moved. Did the noises stop? Eventually ... this would go on for 20 minutes. Paranoid and not feeling well at all, I told my husband to apologize to the ghost so we could get some sleep.

NEXT MORNING-RUBBER DUCKY. After making it through the night, we got up and literally ran out of the room for breakfast. Upon our leaving the villa, I couldn't even look in the livingroom. We drove to the plantation house and enjoyed a nice breakfast in a scenic room.

As we were heading back to the villa, it was my hope that the encounters were over and we could leave the property peacefully. Wrong. Between the footsteps, the television, and the sounds in the bathroom, I was more than frazzled and convinced that we gotten our monies worth staying at Litchfield Plantation. I had also convinced myself that I would probably never step foot on that property again and was intending to swear off ghost hunting due to it being so stressful.

As we returned to our room to pack our things, my husband decides to unlock the porch door from inside our room and go out to look in the backyard (recall it was pitch dark the night before and we couldn't see anything).

In addition to noticing dense trees and hearing a stream, what he also noticed would send me running out of the place. The rubber ducky that was positioned on the hot tub had been moved from it to the other side of the room now sitting on a ledge. He asked me if I had touched it (imagine my expression) ... to which I said ... "NOT." The porch doors (outside and inside) had remained latched with no access. So, how did the rubber ducky get from one side of the room to the other side? Ask the ghost who played in our bathroom.

QUESTIONS AND THOUGHTS

Did someone enter our room while we were at breakfast unlatching the door to the sun porch moving the rubber ducky? No. Could anyone get into the porch from the outside since it was also latched? No.

Rubber duckies don't reposition and move themselves across the room on their own. How do you explain this?

Televisions don't throw sparks out at you like a fireworks display and continue working. How do you explain this?

The sound of an eye pencil is dropped rolling on the floor (no physical movement). How do you explain this?

The sound of a door opening with footsteps walking inside down your foyer with no one to be found. How do you explain this?

Registration desk clerks do not always forewarn their guests that the place is haunted and reminds you that payment is "final."

Who came to visit us that evening? Will never know.

Chapter 4
Clinking Coins - Ghost Maid

Photo Taken by Kelly Renee Schutz
(December 2007)

Bed and Breakfast
Myrtles Plantation, Saint Francisville, Louisiana

Chapter 4
Clinking Coins - Ghost Maid

PHENOMENA AND HISTORY

Twelve ghosts supposedly roam the Myrtles plantation house and property built over a sacred Indian burial ground. One legend, a former slave by the name of Chloe, and perhaps most famous, supposedly poisoned three family members, was punished by being killed by her owner and then, her remains thrown in a river. A ghost of a young Native American woman appears on occasion. Two black shadow children are photographed sitting on the roof of the house. The blood stain of a human body, possibly a former owner, remains in a doorway and will not come clean. A grandfather clock rings at 12:00 midnight with no chimes inside to create a sound.

Union soldiers are reported walking through the General Bradford Suite on their mission somewhere. A ghost maid is seen sweeping the veranda just outside the General Bradford Suite during the early morning hours before dusk. Mr. Winter dies on the seventeenth step inside the house after being shot. And, a haunted mirror positioned on a wall on the first floor in the plantation house hallway is rumored to hold the ghostly souls of Sara Woodruff and two of her children.

The famous Myrtles Plantation located in Saint Francisville, Louisiana, is not only publicly advertised as a "mysterious" bed and breakfast but is one of the most haunted in America.

Photo Taken by Kelly Renee Schutz

HISTORY. The information provided is credited to all the writers who researched the history of Myrtles Plantation. The home, constructed in 1796 (approx. 220 years old as of 2016), is alleged to be rich in historical hauntings.[1]

The Myrtles Plantation was built in 1796 by General David Bradford and was called Laurel Grove. General Bradford lived there alone in exile for several years until President John Adams pardoned him for his role in the Pennsylvania Whiskey Rebellion.[1,2] He then moved his wife Elizabeth and their five children from a plantation they owned in Pennsylvania to it. David Bradford died in 1808.[2] In 1817, one of Bradford's law students, Clark Woodruff (or Woodroff) married Bradford's daughter, Sara Mathilda. Clark and Sara Woodruff managed the plantation for David Bradford's widow, Elizabeth. The Woodruffs had three children: Cornelia Gale, James, and Mary Octavia.[3] Sara Bradford Woodruff and two of her three children died in 1823 and 1824 of yellow fever.[3,4]

When Elizabeth Bradford died in 1831, Clark Woodruff and his surviving daughter Mary Octavia moved to Covington, Louisiana, leaving a caretaker to manage the plantation. In 1834, Woodruff sold the plantation, the land, and its slaves to Ruffin Gray Stirling. Woodruff died in New Orleans in 1851.[3,4]

Stirling and his wife, Mary Catherine Cobb, undertook an extensive remodeling of the plantation house. When completed, the new house was nearly double the size of the former building. They had changed the name to "The Myrtles," named after the Myrtle trees that adorned the property. They imported fancy handcrafted furniture from Europe. The Stirlings had nine children, but five of them died young. Stirling died in 1854 and left the plantation to his wife.[3]

In 1865, Mary Cobb hired William Drew Winter to help manage the plantation as her lawyer and agent. Winter was married to Mary Cobb's daughter, Sarah Stirling. Sarah and William Winter lived at the Myrtles and had six children, one of whom (Kate Winter) died from typhoid fever at the age of three. Although the Winters were forced to sell the plantation in 1868 (due to financial difficulties), they were able to buy it back two years later.[3]

In 1871, William Winter was shot on the porch of the house, possibly by a man named E.S. Webber,[5] and died within minutes after crawling back inside the house and part way up the staircase. Sarah remained at the Myrtles with her mother and siblings until 1878, when she died. Mary Cobb died in 1880, and the plantation passed to Stephen, one of her sons. With the plantation heavily in debt, Stephen sold it in 1886 to Oran D. Brooks. Brooks sold it in 1889, with the house changing hands several times until 1891, when it was purchased by Harrison Milton Williams.[3] In the early part of the 20th century, the land surrounding the house was divided among the heirs of Harrison Milton Williams. In the 1950s, the house itself was sold to Marjorie Munson, who apparently noticed odd things happening around the area surrounding the Myrtles.

The plantation went through several more ownership changes in the 1970s before being bought by James and Frances Kermeen Myers. The Myers ran the plantation as a bed and breakfast. Frances Myers, writing as Frances Kermeen, wrote a book about Myrtles Plantation, naming it as the most haunted house in America.

ALLEGED HAUNTINGS. With the property situated on top of an Indian burial ground, the Myrtles Plantation is alleged to be one of the most haunted bed and breakfasts in the United States. Twelve (12) ghosts supposedly roam the property, with CHLOE, a slave and most famous, as the main draw of visitors and ghost seekers to the property. Ten murders occurred inside the house.[1,2] However, only the one murder, that of William Winter, can be verified through historical records.[2,3] In 2002, *Unsolved Mysteries* presented a documentary about the alleged hauntings at Myrtles.[4,5] According to host Robert Stack, the production crew experienced technical difficulties while filming the segment. It is not uncommon for apparitions [spirits, ghosts] to affect the functioning of camera and video equipment causing malfunctions. Myrtles Plantation was also featured on a 2005 episode of *Ghost Hunters*[1,5] as well as the television show, *Ghost Adventures* (date unknown).

HAUNTED REPORTS. The plantation is reportedly haunted by a young girl who died in 1868, despite being treated by a local voodoo practitioner. She supposedly appears in the room in which she died, and has been reported to practice voodoo on people sleeping in the room.[9] There is also a ghost who reportedly walks, staggers, or crawls up the stairs and stops on the 17th step.[3,10] Some have said that this ghost is that of William Drew Winter, a victim of the only verified murder in the house.[3,10] Mr. Winter was shot on his front porch and, according to legend, staggered or crawled up the stairs but collapsed dead on the 17th step.[3] Alternate versions of his murder claim he managed to crawl up the stairs and collapsed in his wife's arms on the 17th step.[3,10] Regardless of which version is right or wrong, *Ghost Adventures*, conducted an experiment using triggers such as "of age music" and a "plastic kicking ball" to see if any activity would occur on the 17th step. They did show that the triggers of music and ball worked to manifest something that kicked the ball with force right at the video camera. This would indicate an intelligent haunting.

DID CHLOE REALLY EXIST? Perhaps the most well-known tale or legend told of Myrtles Plantation is that of a ghost named, Chloe (Cleo).[6] Chloe was supposedly a slave owned by Clark and Sara Woodruff. It was speculated Mr. Woodruff forced Chloe to become his mistress.[7] A version of the legend of Chloe involved her listening in at keyholes to learn news of Clark Woodruff's business dealings.[7] Upon being caught, Mr. or Mrs. Woodruff cut off one of her ears. From then on, she wore a green turban to hide it.[7]

REVENGE. Further reports and speculation about having her ear cut off turned to her seeking revenge on the Woodruffs by baking a birthday cake and mixing within it, an extract of boiled and reduced oleander leaves (poison). In her attempt to sicken the family, it was also her intent to redeem her position by curing them.[2] However, legend states the poisoning and redemption attempt backfired.[2] Legend also states that Mrs. Woodruff (Sara) and her two daughters ate the cake with all three dying from the poisoning.[2] Historical accounts reported otherwise, with yellow fever as being the cause of their deaths. Chloe was supposedly hanged along with other slaves and thrown into the Mississippi River.[2]

Some historical records do not support these legends. Some records claim the Woodruffs did not own a slave named Chloe (Cleo), or any slaves.[3] Legends also claim Sara and her two daughters were not poisoned but rather died of yellow fever. Legend also claims Mary Octavia (one of the children) survived well into adulthood. Finally, Sara, James [few reports indicated she also had a son], and Cornelia Woodruff were not killed by poisoning, but instead succumbed to yellow fever.[3,7] Regardless, the factual accuracy of the Chloe story has different claims. Some believe she never existed. Some believe a woman wearing a green turban continues to haunt the plantation.[3]

DEFINITIONS

Ghost Lights – mysterious lights that are seen at a distance, usually appearing as blue or yellow spheres, may blink like a candle. Skeptics attribute these lights to swamp gas, magnetism, or electricity. **Haunted House** – a building, a residence of past or present where paranormal activity tends to be witnessed or experienced by more than one person. **Intelligent Haunting** – a haunting by a conscious spirit which interacts with living persons. **Portal** – a location where spirits or entities enter the physical realm.

Residual Haunting – playback of a past event in a continuous loop caused by a trigger or when atmospheric conditions are right. Examples, trauma and tragedy, such as hearing footsteps walking down a hallway or hearing screams. **Sun Flares** – reflections of different sized orbs or half-moon shaped glare, caused and casted from a strong reflection of the sun bouncing off the camera lens.

Haunted Mirror
Photo with Filter Applied by Kelly Renee Schutz

HAUNTED MIRROR. In 2007, a mirror, known as the "haunted mirror" was located on a wall in the Myrtles Plantation home situated on the main floor down a long hallway. It is alleged to hold the spirits of Sara Woodruff and two of her children.[35] The evening my husband and I were on a tour in this home, I believe I photographed a slave (wearing a turban) and a little boy in the mirror. See image on the previous page. A better view of this image can be seen on Trip Advisor, under my name, ghosthunter044 (look up Myrtles Plantation). The boy and the slave appear to be overlapping one another.

ORBS AS INDICATORS. You can see a round orb directly above the perceived "slave and boy." Orbs can indicate a spirit is visually present. A custom of the past was to cover mirrors when a death occurred to not allow the soul of the departed to become absorbed or trapped within. The mirrors of the past use to be lined with silver. Silver was known to absorb energy. This is the reason why people covered their mirrors with a black cloth.

DEBUNKING THE MIRROR

NOT THE ORIGINAL MIRROR. Both times my husband and I were on the Myrtles tours, we were told the haunted mirror was not original to the home or period. It was supposedly purchased at a garage sale to hang in the house for decoration. Many mirrors, during earlier times, were lined with a reflective substance poured directly over the top (silver-like substance) of oil paintings or pictures and then covered in glass. As time goes on, what is beneath the reflective substance begins to show through.

Are the images seen in this mirror ghostly hauntings occurring in the house or someone's relative with a silver overlay not related to this household?

OUR ENCOUNTERS

On December 27, 2007, my husband and I took a trip to Louisiana to stay at the famously advertised, Myrtles Plantation bed and breakfast. Having already stayed at the haunted Litchfield Plantation, you would think our scare there would have put my ghost hunting days to rest. The Myrtles entrance, with its large billboard advertising the property as a mystery, stands proudly on the side of the road boasting its claim. The property is so intriguing that one feels drawn to entering. Legend has it that a gatekeeper watches the entrance informing registered visitors that the property is closed and telling them that they must leave. The gatekeeper than wanders back to its watch hut and disappears. As people complain about his rudeness, they would be informed that no such employee existed. This has happened on more than one occasion. Also, the place is so intriguing that school aged children want to spend their birthday overnights in the house wanting to be spooked.

OUR CHECK-IN. We stayed in the General Bradford Suite (ground level). After obtaining our key from the very well-known, inn-keeper Hester, we proceeded to take a tour first before entering our room. The General Bradford Suite was situated at the end of a veranda outside. Several rocking chairs lined the wooden walkway. A typical tourist trap, many people were roaming the property with cameras and video equipment trying to capture a ghost in "daylight." At Myrtles, anything is possible.

DOOR WOULDN'T OPEN. At approximately 3:00 PM, after the day tour was over, my husband and I proceeded to settle into the General Bradford Suite. We had no problem opening the door on our first attempt. The General Bradford Suite had a parlor room and bedroom connected. Just prior to supper, my husband decided to take a nap while I walked the grounds to take some pictures. It was at the point when I returned that my key would not allow me to open the door. It was as if the key mechanism was stuck and wouldn't allow me to turn the key left or right. Was this a faulty door lock? Or something else trying to keep me out?

As with the Litchfield Plantation door situation, the key issue was the same. I struggled to get the key to turn left and right being unsuccessful in opening the door. I tapped on the door and my husband let me in. At the point where he opened the door, the key moved freely in both directions. Something odd had just happened.

SET OUT DIMES. We left the room around 5:30 PM to eat at a restaurant on the property. We arrived back in time for the 8:00 PM haunted tour. While waiting for the tour to start, my husband went over to the gift shop to buy a book to read. Darkness was upon us with the air filled with an unsettled energy. Upon his return, we set out dimes on our bedroom fireplace mantel ledge hoping for some movement while we were on the ghost tour.

THE SCREAM. Being part of the haunted tour was chilling. As we entered the dining room (low light), we listened to tales about how cups and saucers were found turned upside down and all over the room after the table was nicely set for public display. We viewed the famous picture of Chloe, the ghost woman, who was photographed near the house bringing to this place its profound and famous reputation. We heard tales about how, at times, ghost people would manifest and stand among the tourists during the haunted tours. It was at this point when the guide was about to tell another tale that a tourist accidently leaned up against a light switch and shut off the lights giving all of us the fright of our lives. Having a near collective heart attack, including the tour guide, you could hear a blood curdling SCREAM while we were all standing in a pitch-black room. The tourist apologized (not planned).

PORTAL. In one of the other rooms, the tour guide talked about a portal where someone's dead son appeared standing amongst the group on one side of the room with his mother looking at him from the other side. The mother noticed her dead son and started crying.

The portal room brings a variety of unexplained experiences. A **portal** is a location where spirits can travel through a cavity or tunnel to gain access into the physical world. Sounds far-fetched? Anything is possible at Myrtles Plantation.

BLUE BALL MANIFESTS. As the tourist guide was wrapping up the evening, we were all escorted into a small, dark room at the end of the hallway (across from the grandfather clock that rings at midnight with no means of making a sound). The theme of his ghostly story involved one Halloween evening. Actors would dress up and take people around the dark house with only the actor holding a candle. In one room, the actor was told to stand in one spot, which was behind a dressing screen until asked to come out. While waiting for her cue to come out, she apparently saw a blue ball coming towards her from across the room transforming itself into who she felt was "Chloe" right before her eyes. The ghostly apparition looked left, right, right at her, and then, disappeared. The actor freaked out, her candle blew out, and she crawled on the floor trying to find her way out of the room. Sounds far-fetched? Anything can happen at Myrtles Plantation.

SARAH'S ROOM. Finally, the as the tour guide was giving information in Sarah's room about Myrtles, he reported seeing what looked like children footsteps walking all over the top of the bed next to him. He said he just stood there and watched the feet prints run all over the bedding leaving foot tracks. Sounds far-fetched, doesn't it? Anything can happen at Myrtles Plantation.

BLUE MIST/LIGHTS. Look at the picture on the next page (near the trunk of the tree). What you are unable to see in this black and white picture is a "blue mist" surrounding "ghost lights" inside. I was alone in this area when I took this picture and did not see the lights at the time. No, this isn't a light or sun flare reflecting from my camera lens nor are the lights coming from behind the tree. The blue mist is in front of the tree.

A better image of this picture can be seen on Trip Advisor (my name is ghosthunter044, Myrtles Plantation). The ghost lights are very bright, rod shaped.

Many would argue that what I captured is nothing more than a reflection being cast off by the sun behind the trees or a light situated by the tree. But neither offers a plausible explanation. In my attempt to debunk the image, what you see is a blue mist surrounding rod-shaped, bright lights in front of the tree. Sound far-fetched?

ADVICE ON CAPTURING GHOSTLY MOMENTS. It takes patience to ghost hunt. The best advice I can give is to not expect anything and keep your expectations low allowing the ghosts to come to you.

Photo by Kelly Renee Schutz

STAFF ABANDONS GUESTS. There is nothing more unnerving than being abandoned on a haunted property. At 8:00 PM, all staff depart leaving guests to take care of themselves. It was a dark, quiet, and night to be staying in a creepy old house. My husband and I went to bed Around 10:00 PM. I was too afraid to go to sleep after the haunted tour. Being chicken, I left the light on all night. My husband fell asleep immediately snoring up a storm. Seems like his falling asleep without issue would become a normal occurrence every time we ghost hunt.

COINS CLANKING. However, my husband reported waking up around 3:00 AM and telling me he heard coins clinking (being dropped or played with) in our room (the coins were situated on a fireplace mantel).

KICKED FOOT. He also claimed I kicked his foot with mine in the middle of the night. I asked him how he knew it was my foot since I was hovered to my side of the bed and laid as stiff as a board in fear.

CHILDREN SNUGGLE. There had been numerous reports that one of the deceased children liked to snuggle with guests in this bed and others reported blowing in their ears, vibrating floor, soldiers walking through the room, and a swinging chandelier. Saw and felt nothing.

MAID OUTSIDE OF DOOR. At 5:00 AM, I woke up and looked at my clock. I felt relieved that I made it through the night without incident, or so I thought. That was until I spoke to a ghost hunter roaming the veranda the next morning where she showed me an image of a white, ghostly figure, about 4' feet tall in front of the door to our room around 5:00 AM. Recall I woke up at 5:00 AM.

The ghostly figure was photographed in front of our screen door leading into our suite. Legend states that a "maid" swept the veranda during the morning hours. Although the camera the person used wasn't the best, she did photograph something peculiar that appeared to be the shape of a woman, white'ish glow (semi-bowed dress), about 4' feet tall, doing something. Since I knew how to tell the difference between "fake and real" photograph ... I assured her that what she captured was no defect or back flash (against our door) and was probably the maid. All I could think about was whether this ghost entered our room while we were sleeping. Was it she who played around with the coins? Who kicked my husband's foot? People have been known to leave the property in a panic in the middle of the night never to return. Anything can happen at Myrtles Plantation.

PRIOR GUEST REPORTS. A guest reported being at Myrtles three years prior. She and her husband mocked the idea of ghosts but found themselves packing up in the middle of the night leaving and never returning. Their chandelier began moving in the children's room, where they stayed. One would debate if someone was purposefully swinging the chandelier from above. This is doubtful since there was no room above. There for their 2nd time, she came alone with one of her children to celebrate a birthday party with the husband remaining at home refusing to come back. Anything can happen at Myrtles.

Chapter 5
Kicked In The Air

Illustration by Brandy Woods

The Groveland Hotel at Yosemite National Park
Groveland, California

Chapter 5
Kicked In The Air

PHENOMENA

It had been reported that four ghosts roamed the Groveland Hotel, located just outside of Yosemite National Park, Groveland, California, at will, with two being noticeably active.

Common reports of those most active had been: (1) the ghost of an annoyed gambler either disliked guests for personal reasons or those who snored loudly at night disturbing its sleep. This ghost paid a visit to me when I stayed in the Lavoroni Room (#11) one evening and became annoyed with my snoring thus kicking me from underneath the bed into the air at least 6"-12" upward. This same ghost gambler also liked to clean himself frequently at the sink, lock people in the bathroom, hide men's socks and TV remote under the bed, and flung pictures from the wall onto the bed. And, ... (2) Down the hallway, in Lyle's Room (#15), a miner by the name of Lyle, disliked it when women left their cosmetics out on his dresser. He disliked this so much that he either moved the items to a sink, knocked them onto the floor, or threw them behind the dresser.[2,3] Lyle, on occasion, would go across the road to visit Charlotte, a ghost woman, to spend time with her.

Two other spirits, a young girl and possibly a woman, causes of death unknown, also roamed the property.

HISTORY OF LYLE

In 1927, during Lyle's gold panning days, he died of natural causes in his room leaving a box of dynamite underneath his bed. Being a miner, these were his tools of his trade. His spirit continues to roam the hotel at will.[1,2,3]

Photo by Kelly Renee Schutz
The Groveland Hotel (taken May 2013)

HISTORY OF PROPERTY

The Groveland Hotel, located just outside of Yosemite National Park, is a charming, older property, situated in the mountains. According to Touhy (2016), the Groveland Hotel was originally an adobe trading post built in 1849.[1] Over the years, the building has been a gambling house, saloon, hotel, ranger station, business offices, and a Greyhound bus stop. Known as "the best house on the hill" during the Gold Rush, the hotel may be the only Sierra Nevada Mountain building constructed in the Monterey Colonial architectural style popular during the late 1840's and 1850's.[1]

The building, with its interior stripped, had sat dormant for many years gathering dust and rainwater. Under foreclosure and risking complete demolition, the house was rescued and revitalized by Peggy and Grover Mosley in 1990. They spent two years completing a million-dollar restoration of the property with an adjacent 1914 Queen Anne Victorian building.[1]

DEFINITIONS

Agent – a living person who is the focus of poltergeist activity. **Assaultive Poltergeist** – biting, scratching, pinching, pulling hair, pushing, etc. **Authentication** – proving genuine verification of facts surrounding an occurrence of paranormal phenomena. **Benign Spirit** – a spirit that is not harmful. **Chance** – random, unpredictable influences on events. **Earthbound** – ghost or spirit that is unable to cross over at the time of death. **Intelligent Haunting** – interaction on the physical plane as in communication or object movement from a spirit who is conscious. **Levitation** – to lift or raise a physical object in apparent defiance of gravity. **Place-Centered Haunting** – a location where paranormal events frequently take place. **Poltergeist** – non-human entity (noisy ghost) usually more malicious or destructive than ghosts or deceased human beings. May involve thumping, banging, levitation or movement of objects, stone throwing, and starting fires.[4] **Touched** – the act of having physical contact from a spirit or entity [paranormal investigation or otherwise] such as pulling hair, shirt tugging, pushing, etc.

QUESTIONS AND THOUGHTS

Is Groveland, California prone to earthquakes or plate tectonic movement? No. Could the mining of silver in the hills and mountains surrounding Groveland be a conductor of energy to manifest ghostly activity? Yes. Silver is a metal that absorbs energy and ghosts need energy to manifest. Could the energy from traumatic events of those involved in shoot outs and murder remain in buildings and surrounding area? Yes. Energy can also be absorbed into walls, stone, and metal. What were the weather conditions the night I was kicked into the air while sleeping in the The Lavoroni Room? Crystal clear sky allowing for a strong energy field to aid in manifestation.

ENCOUNTER - KICKED IN THE AIR

The encounter I had with an annoyed gambler [ghost] that haunted our room while staying at the Groveland Hotel will always be one of my most memorable experiences.

It was around the beginning of the second week in May 2013 when my husband and I took an adventurous trip out West. As part of this trip, we made a temporary stop at Mission Community College, where I had interviewed for a teaching position. We began our driving adventure by leaving Las Vegas proceeding through Burbank, California, Pismo Beach, Rio Del Mar Beach (near Santa Monica), and traveling up a L-O-N-G ... windy, steep mountain to reach our destination, The Groveland Hotel (near Yosemite National Park). Here, we stayed at this publicly known haunted hotel for one night. Disappointed that we were not able to stay in Lyle's room, I was hopeful that in hearing about other reported deaths on the property that we might have some type of experience. And, I am happy to report – WE DID.

The town of Groveland extends a few blocks in either direction and is small not offering much for food, rest, or entertainment. After checking into our room, we went to have dinner next door at a very run down (but charming) saloon converted into a restaurant called the "Iron Door Saloon" (built in 1852). With its aged interior and entire ceiling littered with dollar bills stuck to it (people would take a pin, stick it through a bill, and throw it up to the ceiling hoping it would stick), we enjoyed the character and ambiance of this place. After eating, we went back to our room and stepped out onto the balcony to admire the quiet town, full moon, and smell the crisp, fresh air.

Photo by Kelly Renee Schutz
Bed and Sink – The Lavoroni Room #11

JOURNAL ENTRIES. When we came back into our room from the balcony, I began to read entries written in a journal in our room from those who had stayed there before us. I was shocked to learn that our room (Lavoroni) was as haunted as Lyle's room. We had heard stories from staff about other ghosts who roamed the property but their stories did not appear to be "the talk of the place."

One thing mentioned in a pamphlet located in the lobby was that it if the premises appeared to be quiet (no ghostly happenings), that Lyle had a tendency to go across the road to a hotel to visit a woman ghost by the name of Charlotte.

Exhausted, we settled in for the evening attempting to go to sleep. It just so happens that when I am very tired, I snore loudly. I had asked my husband to put his socks out to see if the ghost would be triggered into hiding them under the bed (previous reports).

THE MOMENT OF BEING KICKED. My husband had no problem sleeping (as usual). It was about 2:23 AM when I awoke (startled) to find myself bouncing on the bed having been kicked from underneath into the air. It was like something had shoved its foot underneath my back and pushed upward. Because I bounced onto the bed, it felt to me that I may have been airborne approximately 6" to 12" (straight up). Startled by what had just happened to me, I immediately looked at the clock and then, turned to my side to see if my husband was also kicked but he was sound asleep. I looked toward the sink because the gambler was known for continuous hand-washing but I saw nothing near me. I tried to wake my husband but he would not wake up. It was as if he were in a trance-like sleep. I have seen him in these states of sleep before in several situations where I just had or am having a paranormal encounter.

After shaking him vigorously, he woke up but what had been in that room had vanished. Or was the ghostly apparition still there "under the bed"?

ONE OTHER BED SHAKING OCCURRENCE. The next day, I read every page in the journal hoping to find a similar story to mine. I found one entry from a couple of years back stating the bed was shaken vigorously during the middle of the night with snoring being mentioned. What is most interesting is how the ghost in this room likes to take men's socks and the TV remote and hide them directly under the bed. With the bed frame space 2-3 inches from the floor, it is puzzling how these items end up directly underneath.

From a paranormal perspective, when things go missing or are moved ... the entity has issue with it. Either wants it for itself. Trying to hide it in a game-like situation. Or, wants to let someone know that he/she is not alone (wants attention).

CHECK-OUT. At check-out, I asked the receptionist if the area was prone to earthquakes to which the answer was "no." At this point, the staff began to beam with happiness when I told them I had a visitor in my room who didn't like a snoring guest. My encounter was the buzz for the day, gaining hype from everywhere.

Apparently, no reports of Lyle or any other ghost sighting had been brought to their attention for several months. It was at the point that we were saying goodbye when a couple walked into the building and sarcastically made a request, "we would like to stay in the haunted room" (he-he-ha-ha) ... to which I responded, "would you like to stay in our room? I was kicked up into the air last night about a foot off the bed." Both of their faces turned white. I am not a small woman and to lift me seemed effortless to this ghost.

The morale of the story -- never underestimate the force and strength of any annoyed entity. In the end, after the dust settled, this remains in my top five as one of my best experiences interacting with something paranormal that didn't try to hurt me. It could have been worse – the entity could have thrown me off the bed in any direction.

Chapter 6
Choked in Bed

Illustration by Brandy Woods

Chapter 6
Choked in Bed

PHENOMENA

You have heard the expression, "when things go bump in the night." Have you ever heard of this saying? "When things choke you in the middle of the night?" I believe we had an active **portal** in one of our first homes. This **portal** was situated underneath the foundation located directly under our livingroom floor stationed beneath the placement of our glass-top, wood frame coffee table. This **portal** brought various entities (positive and negative) into our home. Many of these entities had their own character, behavior issues, and agendas. Numerous situations escalated in our seventh year living in this house with frequent taunting of both of us by the time we left in our eighth year living there.

NEW HOME BRINGS SPOOKY GUESTS

My husband and I have lived all over the United States and Canada in several homes. During one of our moves, we purchased a newer one-owner home that was approximately 10 years old.

We had lived in this home for nearly seven of eight years when we began noticing that the energy and environmental conditions were changing. Thinking we might have brought an apparition home with us from one of our travels (also known as an "attachment"), I purchased a K-2 meter and began monitoring our house for signs of energy spikes. I also purchased a motion sensor and aimed it in various directions to scan for movement.

WARNING: What I did not know then and was informed as of this writing from experts in the field ... K2 meters are about as bad as Ouija boards. They tend to draw the entities through them and into your environment. The rule of thumb is to never turn one on in your own home.

DEFINITIONS

Agent – a living person who is the focus of poltergeist activity. **Assaultive Poltergeist** – biting, scratching, pinching, pulling hair, pushing, choking, etc. **Attachment** – tagging along or following a person from its place of origin. **Attacked** – a form of physical or emotional distress caused onto the target person, such as hurting the person physically (scratches and bruises), making the person physically ill, causing a sense of being dazed or dizzy. **Intelligent Haunting** – interaction on the physical plane as in communication or object movement from a spirit who is conscious. **Poltergeist** – non-human entity (noisy ghost) usually more malicious or destructive than ghosts or deceased human beings. May involve thumping, banging, levitation or movement of objects, stone throwing, and starting fires. **Portal** – a location where spirits or entities enter the physical realm.

SLEEP PARALYSIS

Sleep paralysis is defined as "a feeling of being conscious but unable to move."[1] This condition occurs when a person passes between the stages of wakefulness and sleep. During these situations, a person may be unable to move or speak for a few seconds up to a few minutes. Some people may also feel pressure or a sense of choking. Sleep paralysis usually occurs either while falling asleep, called hypnagogic or pre-dormital sleep paralysis or when waking up, called hypnopompic or post-dormital sleep paralysis.[1]

OUR ENCOUNTERS

When one moves into a home, it takes a few months to adjust to its sounds and smells. Up until our seventh year living in this home, we noticed nothing out of the ordinary. It was during our seventh year that something felt a bit strange. The first thing we noticed (more than one occasion) that seemed odd to us was the behavior of our neighbor's cat, who came over frequently, was playing with an invisible "something" in our backyard. We then began noticing a dog from a few doors down coming to our front door, then proceeding to go around to our backyard looking as if it were following an invisible "something." I would point out this behavior to my husband making a comment that the animals appeared to be playing with invisible friends.

EVENTS INSIDE HOUSE. Months later, we would notice strange occurrences inside our house.

HAIR AND LEGS. The first observance was that of my arm hair and legs standing on end every time I went upstairs to a specific room on the 2nd floor. On various occasions, it would feel as if I was walking through a magnetic field. Some might argue that what I felt was a build-up of static electricity on the carpet; however, this feeling only happened entering one area to one specific room.

TELEPHONE. The second observance would be that of our landline telephone that would blink indicating someone was on the phone when no one was on the phone. Static would be heard when picked up to listen.

WATER BOTTLE CAP. The third observance would be that of an untouched water bottle cap shooting off the bottle without warning on the coffee table.

SPOON SPINNING. The fourth observance would be that of my watching a spoon spinning around inside a small Ben & Jerry's ice cream cup by itself (very fast).

TAPPING. The fifth observance would be tapping on our kitchen cupboards (knock-knock) wanting to get my attention and when ignored, would make the sound of a large water drinking glass dropped behind my head on our sofa table while I was trying to watch TV. There was no drinking glass, just the sound of it. This unexpected sound made me jump about a foot into the air.

CHRISTMAS ORNAMENT. The sixth observance would be that of a sound of a Christmas ornament falling to the ground breaking. What was happening during this event was that the entity was trying to lure me into the livingroom. I never went into the livingroom – I ignored it.

THERMOMETER. The seventh occurrence would be that of a thermometer plaque on our bathroom wall found crooked (just like you see in a cartoon). No one touched it.

HUSBAND POSSESSED. The eighth and most troubling was when my husband acted strangely talking oddly (like he was possessed by something).

ARGUMENTS. This episode led to an eruption of unexplained arguments between us when we never fought and to this day, still never fight.

BEDROOM. Finally, my using my motion sound sensor and K-2 meter to discover that what may have been taunting us seemed to enjoy sitting in the middle of our master bedroom bed. The entity was intelligent enough to hold a lengthy conversation with me when I used my ghost radar conversation application to ask questions of it getting intelligent responses.

EVENTS ISOLATED TO SPECIFIC LOCATIONS. These events convinced me that we had one or more visitors in our house, one that we referred to as "Ben." Over time, we isolated the incidents to four areas in our home: (1) our master bedroom bed on the first level, (2) our master bathroom, (3) our coffee table in our livingroom, and (4) one of our 2nd floor bedrooms. We felt we had a portal beneath the coffee table underneath our foundation in our livingroom (right side bottom corner) that allowed unknown entities to enter our house. For months, we lived in what we thought was harmony with many of these unseen ghost(s) until one evening, I encountered a threat to my life.

CHOKED TO GASPING. Many paranormal events happen during a new or full moon phase (three days before, during, and three days after) due to the energy field being at its strongest during these periods of time. This is especially true during a clear sky evening. One full moon evening, the mood in our house would change from calm to aggressive.

With my husband in a deep sleep, I would find myself awakened around 2:30 AM by something that had its hands around my neck choking me to the point where I needed to gasp for air. This would happen on two separate occasions. Was I having a sleep apnea attack? Was this my thyroid acting up? Could this have been sleep paralysis? Was this something trying to get my attention? Or, was this entity trying to kill me. The question of course … why? Since those incidents, I have never had another like it (4-5 years later to date).

If it were sleep apnea or paralysis, I would imagine I would have had more episodes. However, I have not and could feel hands around my neck. This also reminds me of one or two times when I was awakened by something screaming in my ear. Like a loud witch scream. I wonder if in those situations if they were related to a demonic "hag" trying to scare me.

GHOST RETALIATES. With all of the unexpected occurrences building up with intensity over time in our house, my being choked on more than one occasion while sleeping in bed, my husband appearing to be possessed by something during his illness moments, and my capturing the entity in at least four locations in our home, with the most specific location being in the MIDDLE of our bed, I felt it was time to pack up our things, sell our home, and find a new one. Our decision to move brought yet another situation with the ghost resident, its retaliation for our leaving.

VICTORIAN FIXTURE GLOBE. On the day of moving, I was in the house alone. I had just placed securely on our kitchen island an antique light fixture globe that had Victorian roses painted on it. I did not know of its age when I acquired it from my grandparents but knew it must have been at least 65 years old. This globe came from their house that had that negative entity behind the curtain. Prior to it being gifted to me, it had sat on a shelf in their kitchen for years. When we had moved into our second house, we created a special location for it in our master bedroom closet. To that point, I had cherished the safety of this globe no matter where we moved.

GLOBE DROPS BEHIND MY BACK. In my efforts to pack my car one evening in anticipation of our move, I recall placing the globe on the kitchen island in a safe location so it would not roll off onto the floor. As I grabbed something from the island to bring to my car, I no sooner than turned around when I heard something "crash" onto the floor. I knew at that moment that this entity was upset with my moving effort and pushed it off the island on purpose. When the globe hit the floor, it remained wrapped inside a painter cloth I had placed around it. Due to its age, it broke into pieces but did not scatter as it fell onto the floor. I picked up the broken globe pieces and with no emotion, threw the entire globe into the trash. I said out loud to the entity, "feel better now?" "You know that globe meant the world to me." Coincidence? No.

HOUSE FALLING APART. This would not be the only odd occurrence we experienced while packing up our things. Light bulbs (new) would suddenly burn out, door handles would fall off, and odds and ends would need repair delaying our ability to prepare the house for a final inspection. It had appeared the house was falling apart. And, what a coincidence – ON MOVING DAY. Showing no emotion during these events, we told the entity to remain in the house and to not follow us to our new location.

<u>QUESTIONS / THOUGHTS</u>

How do entities travel through portals? It is obvious they glide through an open channel or crack but why is it that they need this type of entry to move around or manifest? Where do these entities come from? At this specific property, do I feel we experienced ghost animals? Yes. What about the choking incident – was this sleep paralysis or a demonic paranormal attack? I contend that it was a paranormal event instigated by "the hag" or an unseen territorial force. In both cases, not a happy apparition but one that was demonic in nature causing a lot of grief and escalating events.

Chapter 7
Voices – The Love Affair

Photo by Kelly Renee Schutz

Bed and Breakfast
Macdonald Norwood Hall Hotel, Aberdeen, Scotland
(May 2015)

Chapter 7
Voices – The Love Affair

PHENOMENA

The love affair. After years of torment, Mr. James Ogston's wife and mistress each wanted Mr. James Ogston to leave the other but the Mister refused. It has been reported that the Macdonald Norwood Hall Hotel is haunted by the two lovers (Mister and Mistress) and the vengeful wife (Mrs.) who longs for revenge for the torrid years she had to endure from her husband. Love is not so patient or kind.

HISTORY

According to an article written by Haunted Rooms (2016), guests have reported active hauntings coming from the older section of the Macdonald Norwood Hall Hotel in Room1 (ghostly Mistress resides), Room 4 (ghostly Mr. James Ogston resides), Room 8 (our guest room), and Kitchen (ghostly Mrs. James Ogston).[1] These rooms are located at the top of a stairway. Pictures hanging in the dining room of the Mistress and Mister continually stare at each other while a light bulb positioned in a fixture to the right of the fireplace frequently burns out.

It is believed that James originally purchased Norwood in 1872 and rebuilt it in 1881 for his mistress so they could meet while he lived in Ardoe House across the river with his young family.[1]

Haunted Rooms (2016) also reveals that the apparition of James has been seen standing in front of the log fire in the dining room.[1] The ghost of his mistress has been reported to haunt the main stair case (perhaps looking for her lover). His wife is the most active of the three with reports of her being seen in the hallway, the kitchen, and the dining room.[1]

PRIOR HISTORY. In 1861, Mrs. Helen Morrison, wife of Baillie William Adamson (a London stockbroker) bought the property of Norwood. Mr. Adamson liked the name of Norwood and gave it to the house that he built on the land his wife had purchased.[2]

Mrs. Morrison then sold the property to John Taylor of Regent's Park just two years later. It was then later resold again in 1872 to a Colonel James (Soapy) Ogston, who partly rebuilt the house in 1881 before moving his family across the River Dee to Ardoe House and moving his mistress into Norwood.[2]

On the grounds of Norwood is where the ancient Pitfodels Castle once stood.[1] The foundation is likely still there but no remains of the house have been seen for the last fifty years.[2]

DEFINITIONS

Agent – a living person who is the focus of poltergeist activity. **Clairaudience** – an auditory form of ESP, paranormal information is received outside the range of normal perception through voices, whispers, and auditory impressions. **Entity** – anything that has a separate, distinct existence, though not necessarily material in nature. **Hallucination** – vivid perception of sights and sounds not physically present (associated with altered state of consciousness). **Haunting** – reoccurring ghostly phenomena that returns to a location where no one is physically present. **Place-Centered Haunting** – a location where paranormal events frequently take place. **Poltergeist** – non-human entity (noisy ghost) usually more malicious than ghosts or deceased human beings. May involve thumping, banging, levitation or movement of objects, stone throwing, and starting fires.

THE ENCOUNTER

On May 18, 2015, my husband and I stayed at the Macdonald Norwood Hall Hotel, Aberdeen, Scotland for one night. Upon our arrival, we made a request to be moved from the newer section of the hotel to the older section (known to be the most haunted). My husband and I stayed in Room 8 that was located near the top of the staircase. We were drawn to stay at the Macdonald Norwood Hotel after reading that it had an occasional haunting.

Illustration by Brandy Woods

Dead tired (no pun intended) upon arriving from our transatlantic airplane flight, we drove to this hotel, checked in, took a brief walk down the driveway admiring the property, and then, proceeded to go to supper at their in-house restaurant. Just after supper, we had a brief tour by a staff member of the public spaces within the hotel, learning of its history and of its resident ghosts. We went back to our room to settle in for the evening. It just so happens that I was too tired to set up my ghost equipment that evening and told my husband that I would have to simply "waive" my ghost hunting experience. I fell asleep quickly.

THE INCIDENT. Around 1:15 a.m.-1:30 a.m., my husband was awakened suddenly by "something" that sounded like a male voice calling out his name. He awoke in a panic (heart beating) looking around to see if someone was in our room. He saw no one. It was at the point when he heard his name called out that a loud THUMP or BANG sounded on the wall right next to him. Being curious, he went to the door, looked out into the hallway, saw no one on the stairs or in the area. Unusual for him, he remained terrified about that experience still talking about well into the next morning.

REPORTED NEXT MORNING. It was reported to us by staff that next morning that the Mistress' room and Mr. room were at the top of the stairs (Room 1 and Room 4). We didn't know this at the time we were assigned to our room. We only knew that we were in the most haunted section of the hotel. It was also reported that the Mistress liked to frequent the stairs while the Mrs. liked to hang out in the kitchen. The Mr. and Mistress pictures hung in the dining room staring at each other. Their romance continued beyond death.

QUESTIONS AND THOUGHTS

Can owners who once lived at a property return in spirit even if they have been away from this home for a very long time? Yes. Places of comfort can attract the return of former residents. In this case, the Mister gave to the Mistress, the house as a gift. Why is the picture of Mrs. Ogston not hanging in the dining room next to the pictures of the Mistrss and Mr. Ogston? Not clear.

Who exactly called out my husband's name? Not clear. A male sounding voice. Could my husband have been experiencing REM sleep when he heard his name and thump in the wall? No. How do I know this? It was how he described the incident. When the THUMP occurred on the wall next to him, how does one not know that the sound was nothing more than a pipe clanking? My husband described hearing his name and the thump sound at the exact same time. Both together made this experience unusual and coincidental.

Chapter 8
Ectoplasmic Orbs - Nanny-Kids

Illustration by Brandy Woods
Airth Castle and Hotel, Stirlingshire, United Kingdom

Chapter 8
Ectoplasmic Orbs - Nanny-Kids

PHENOMENA

Airth Castle and Hotel is said to have its share of ghosts with several of its rooms presumed to be haunted.[4] The most well-known ghost on location at the castle is that of a 17th century nanny. She is believed to have failed to look after two children who were in her care but died tragically in a fire. She now stalks the castle trying to find the children.[4] Other ghosts include an unseen dog and a maid who screams at night. In 2005, *Ghost Finders Scotland* conducted an investigation of Airth Castle. They detected unusual electromagnetic fluctuations and numerous light anomalies while the group's psychic medium sensed the presence of many spirits.[4]

HISTORY AND HAUNTS

According to an account attributed to Blind Harry, in 1298 a previous wooden fortification on this site was attacked by William Wallace in order to rescue his imprisoned uncle, a priest from Dunipace.[1] A later castle was destroyed after the defeat of King James III at Sauchieburn in 1488.[1] The southwest tower is the earliest part of the castle dating to the period immediately thereafter. An extension was added on the east side in the mid-16th century.[1] Airth Castle was owned by the Bruces, who were

Jacobite sympathizers forced to sell their property after the failure of the 1715 rebellion.[1]

HAUNTS. The Airth castle is a major historic building retaining much medieval fabric. It is designated as a Category A listed building by Historic Scotland.[2] Within the castle grounds stand the ruins of the former parish church of Airth.[2] The castle is said to be haunted by these types of incidents: (1) nanny wandering the castle to locate two young children who were once in her care; (2) sound of playing children can be heard in rooms 3, 4, 9 and 23; (3) people reporting hearing cries and screams believed to be from a maid who was attacked by her master; (4) ghost dog, who likes to bite the ankles of guests roaming the hallways;[3,4] and, (5) grounds man haunts the lower floor of the castle.[1,2,3,4]

DEFINITIONS

Agent – a living agent who is the focus of poltergeist activity. **Anomaly** – an irregular and unusual event that does not follow a standard rule or law or that cannot be explained by scientific theories. **Contact Session** – a period of time in which paranormal investigators attempt to establish communication with an entity. **Ectoplasm** – an immaterial or ethereal substance associated with spirit manifestations (often photographed as fog-like mist, white masses, or vortexes).

Ghost – a form of apparition or supernatural entity (visual appearance of a deceased human spirit). **Infrared Camera** – a camera with incorporated infra-red technology that allows for sensitive imaging (camera or videorecorder) in low light conditions. **Intelligent Haunting** – an interaction with an entity on the physical plane, including object movement or touching. **Investigation** – a carefully controlled research in which various methods and equipment are used to seek confirmation of reports of ghosts or hauntings. **Mist** – a photographed anomaly that appears as a blanket of light or expansion of an orb.

Orb – can represent the spirit of a deceased person or animal often appearing as a ball of light not usually seen visually. Has differing characteristics such as size, color, density, shape, motion, and flexibility. Origins of cause for false orbs = dust, moisture, insects, lens reflection. **Percipient** – person who sees (perceives) an apparition. **Reciprocal Apparition** – rare type of spirit phenomenon in which both the agent and the percipient are able to see and respond to each other.

ENCOUNTER

On May 21, 2015, my husband and I checked into Airth Castle and Hotel in early evening. There are actually two separate buildings on this property that are rented to guests. The newer hotel has modern rooms and the other building, the castle, has updated rooms. Most guests are assigned to stay in the newer hotel that is located about a block away from the castle. At check-in, we made a request to stay in one of the haunted rooms in the castle. We were fortunate to have been granted a room and was assigned to Room 23. It just so happens that when we arrived to settle into our castle room, no staff were present to watch over it during the day or evening. Guests were alone to roam the halls in finding their rooms. We were told most people who knew of the castle's haunted history did not want to stay overnight in it.

In writing my review for Trip Advisor (ghosthunter044) about our experience there, I had provided so many details about what happened to us that they refused to allow my entry unless I made significant changes to it. My entry was rewritten.

OUR EVENING. After check-in, we went over to the castle to find our room. I recall a gathering had been going on at the time in one of the main level ballrooms making it difficult to determine which doors went to guest rooms and which led to other common areas.

Photo by Kelly Renee Schutz
(See Arrows – Room 23 – Our Room Bottom Level)

RATTLING FLOOR BOARDS. We began opening closed doors inside the foyer to attempt to locate the one that would lead us to our room, which ironically, brought us down into a basement. With hesitation, my thought at this point was to turn back and leave. We initially proceeded down carpeted stairs eventually taking us into a narrow hallway that presented itself as a spooky maze. With each of our footsteps shifting as we walked on the loose floor boards, we stumbled in front of our bedroom door.

BEDROOM #23. Upon entrance into our room, the only thing that really greeted us at the time was a wasp flying around in our bathroom. After my husband saved me from it, we settled in for an uneventful hour. Shortly thereafter, we proceeded to get ready to go to dinner leaving the castle and walking up the road to the main hotel. After dinner, we headed back to our castle room, first wanting to explore the castle by opening some of the closed doors on the main floor and sneaking a peek at some of the common areas, such as the ballroom. My initial reaction and feeling was "uneasiness" and "intrigue." As we roamed further, we looked down two long hallways. My gut instinct then was to turn around and simply get out of the building. We decided to stop roaming and proceeded to the basement to our room.

LATER ON - ROOM 23. It was between 10:45 PM and 11:00 PM when we were settling into our room for the evening. I cannot recall the moon phase that evening. My husband likes to read, so he went to the sitting room for a period of time. I took out my ghost equipment (K2 meter, infrared video camera) and was very calm getting myself ready for whatever may have lied ahead.

SITTING ON BED. Sitting on the bed, I no sooner than opened my video camera screen when immediately and right in front of me, I saw in my video viewer, two or three orbs zipping around in a fast flying motion (left to right, right to left). The orbs were not entirely solid, white in color, small round circular masses. At one point, one of the orbs expanded itself in front of me into a somewhat larger mass, showing its capability to spread out from a circular ball to something that appeared flatter.

VIDEO RECORD BUTTON PRESSED. Shaken and scared, I tried to remain calm calling to my husband that we had "visitors." I pressed the video record button and started talking to the orb anomalies trying to keep them there so I could get footage on my camera. At one point, one of the orbs DODGED directly at my camera as if it were going to attack me. It then spread out its ball of light into a flatter mass (mist appearance) and departed through the heavy wooden bedroom door. The other orbs followed it out of the door.

For those of you who have watched the show, *Ghost Adventures* on television, when they show orbs in motion, this is exactly what I saw in front of me. However, I saw two or three at the same time.

FOOTAGE IS ERASED. Thinking I had captured something fantastic on video, I immediately asked my husband to come out of the sitting room to view what I had captured. I was shaking as I wound back the video to show him my footage. It just so happens that although the record button was on for at least 5 minutes, my video captured NOTHING. I recalled the moment when that one orb came at me like it wanted to attack me.

MY EVIDENCE WAS GONE. How can a record button be on for 5 minutes and get nothing imprinted? Ask my orb visitors. I had heard of this before in stories told by other ghost investigators who reported that their equipment sometimes failed in strong activity situations. To date, I remain devastated by the loss of my evidence.

ORB VISITORS COME BACK. I went to bed depressed. I tried for the next hour to get my video camera to work again but with no luck. It was probably around 12:00 AM – 1:30 AM when I was lying in bed hoping the ghost visitors would come back. Well, they did come back and decided to play with my husband's computer by turning it "on-off-on-off-on-off." Keep in mind, at this point, I was very angry they erased my footage. Not being able to get my camera to work the second time around and annoyed by their tactics, I got up from the bed, went over to the computer, told them to knock it off and leave, and pulled the cord out of the wall. I slept with the lights on all night. My husband, as usual, was sound asleep AND not able to awaken when the ghost activity was occurring in the room. An interesting side note, my video camera began functioning properly the next morning. Demonstrates the intelligence and decision making of apparitions if they do not want you to capture anything.

AMAZING EXPERIENCE. What I witnessed was perhaps the most amazing orb motion show I could ever expect to see. My disappointment in not being able to record the visit only allows me to tell you about it. My husband can vouch for the shaking in my voice when I initially saw them. I think he was too afraid to come out of the sitting room because he didn't want to scare them off or vice versa. Being "nice" to the orb visitors doesn't mean anything to them. When I saw the orbs pass through the heavy wooden door, this was one of the most unbelievable moments etched in my memory forever.

The next day, there was no activity in the room. I am not certain if there was a full moon that evening that allowed for a good energy field of the orb experience at the Airth Castle. I have always known myself to be a pied piper that attracts children to me. My feeling is that my encounter in this room involved at least two children (due to their excited, fast moving motion behavior) and perhaps, the nanny, who seemed to be the leader having the ability to not only expand into a larger mist but direct the others in leaving the room. Very active room.

QUESTIONS AND THOUGHTS

How do you know if these anomalies will hurt you or damage your equipment? You don't. This is why you need to wear a cross and say a prayer of protection. Can orb anomalies erase video footage? Yes. It was obvious to me these orb anomalies not only had a form of intelligence but also the ability to affect electrical objects.

Chapter 9
The Farmstead Children

Photo Illustration by Kelly Renee Schutz

Chapter 9
The Farmstead Children

PHENOMENA

You move from a house that became haunted with negative energy forces into a house that shows signs of being haunted. A dead clock's hands start to move during new and full moon evenings. A key in the front door is turned as if something were wanting to lock it to secure your protection. A music box chimes on a stormy lightning filled night. Something scratches the top of your duvet comforter and pulls your sheet down toward the floor with no explanation. Objects are moved and found elsewhere in your home. Food that is sealed in airtight plastic topped containers are sliced open. Pillow cases are found to be pulled back or removed from their pillows.

You attempt to make contact by using your ghost communication application on your device and get the words ... BARN – AFRAID – PROPERTY – BEHIND – ANGRY. You realize the only barn in the area is the one across the road from you. During a fireplace cleaning visit in your home, the service person tells you that you live across the road from a haunted farmstead with its barn remaining as a fragment of an unsettled history. You learn the husband (civil war period) went crazy and killed his wife and children with an ax. You also learn the area you moved into has numerous reports of paranormal activity.

HISTORY OF FARMSTEAD

Across the road from your former haunted property (that you felt you escaped from), brings you right back to an area that appears to have a lot of unexplained paranormal activity. Once farmland, you purchase a home in an upscale neighborhood thinking you are free from paranormal activity. Only to learn from the former owner that a large quarry use to be in your area (with one still active a few miles down the road).

The land your home resides on was developed into a housing subdivision. The sand and/or quartz in the land underneath the homes fuel manifestations with most owners not talking about or recognizing odd occurrences shown to them.

What remains of the farm across the road "to date" is a barn, a silo, and large field. See image next page. The house that sat next to the barn was torn down not only due to a fire but the owner's inability to keep renters for more than a month or two at a time (reports of unexplained hauntings inside and outside of the house).

You see groups of people at the farm on occasion. You suspect it is a paranormal group as there is no other explanation for the visit. Cops regularly sit at the edge of its road either watching for speeders or awaiting an unwelcomed visitor. Dogs bark late at night – what are they barking at? A coyote or something else?

Does this property look haunted to you?

MURDERS AND OTHERS

Little is known about the reason why the father killed his family (civil war days). Legend says he went crazy and killed his wife and children with an ax. With the house torn down, it was presumed the spirits of the murdered children either hide in the barn or take refuge in a house nearby where they seek protection from their mean father.

Finding me across the road was of no surprise. It seems I have a knack for attracting children, animals, and lost souls. And, for some reason, these deceased entities find comfort being near me. With the guidance of one of my ghost experts, she claimed it was also likely that in addition to the ghost children from across the road, that an elderly man, who use to live in the area, and a ghost cat and dog, that lived or visited our property, frequented our home. Verified.

UPDATE: On August 25, 2016, I verified with a former owner of our home some of the happenings we had been experiencing. Keep reading.

DEFINITIONS

Agent – a living person who is the focus of poltergeist activity. **Asport** – a physical object that a spirit teleports to another location or makes disappear. **Contact Session** – period of time in which paranormal investigators attempt to establish communication with an entity. **Earthbound** – a ghost or spirit that was unable to cross over to the other side at the time of death and is stuck in this physical plane. **Entity** – anything that has a separate, distinct existence, though not necessarily material in nature. **Haunting** – reoccurring ghostly phenomena that returns to a location where no one is physically present. **Intelligent Haunting** – an interaction on the physical plane as in communication or object movement. **Moon Phases** – people associate full moons with episodes of paranormal activity. A full moon is most favorable to ghost hunt because the energy fields are at their strongest. The best time to experience paranormal phenomena is two to three days before, during, or after a full moon or new moon. **Place-Centered Haunting** – a location where paranormal events frequently take place. **Touched** – the act of having physical contact from a spirit or entity such as pulling hair, shirt tugging, pushing, scratching, or bruising.

FIRST ENCOUNTERS

EAR BUZZ. My first indication of a ghostly visitor was when I was home alone one night, sitting on the couch, and out of nowhere came a very loud buzzing sound that was rattling in my ear causing my ear drum to hurt. Not having something like this happen to me before, my general reaction was to rub my ear, swat at what I thought was a flying insect, and look around for the cause. I discovered nothing in the room near me. It is not normal for my ear drum to experience high pitched buzzing sounds. Though I experience ringing in my ears frequently, this was not the same. It was at this point that I felt dizzy and sick to my stomach as if my head were in a drum. I should have recognized the cues about having a ghostly encounter near me since my memory was no stranger to flashbacks from my childhood days when staying at my grandparent's home alone brought similar experiences. Add to this, all the odd encounters at my former home – just across the road. However, since I now lived in a nice subdivision, I passed this experience off as anxiety as being in an unfamiliar place. I was wrong.

TINGLING IN ANKLES. This episode led to another situation where one evening while I was sitting in the same location on the couch, I felt an intense tingling radiating through both of my ankles as if something were passing directly through them at the same time. Never experiencing this feeling before, I once again passed this moment off as having an ankle circulation problem. Wrong.

MAKING CONTACT. That episode led into contact with "something" indicating cues on my ghost application program (ability to communicate with ghosts) while my husband and I were painting in one of our bedrooms. Using my ghost application, the words BARN and SCARED came up. At the time, I never paid much attention to the fact that the "barn" it was referring to was across the road from us. I discounted the ghost application words as being random and chalked them up as a mere coincidence of words that meant nothing. Well, those words meant something.

MOON PHASES BRING ENCOUNTERS

Our making adjustments moving into an unfamiliar home brought with it getting use to home settling sounds, feeling pockets of air movement, and hearing neighborhood noises. As a few months went by, I began to think about the "coincidences" I had encountered during our first month living at our new residence. These coincidences would soon turn into episodes I suspected were hauntings. Haunting noises were noticed the most when the month experienced varying moon phases such as a new moon or regular cycling full moons such as blood and super moons.

Illustration by Brandy Woods

CLUES OF ARRIVAL AND DEPARTURE. Our encounters with our ghostly visitors varied with the amount of attention they needed from us. What was certain was when a ghost visitor came and left, it had left us a clue of its being there. The main clue often involved moving the hands on the anniversary clock that had a dead battery or my clock next to my bed. These episodes always occurred during a new moon, full moon, or lightning storm. Here were some of the obvious clues upon ghostly arrivals and departures:

(1) Hands on the anniversary clock would move to different time positions as many as 3-6 hours ahead or backwards.

(2) The key in the front door would be moved from a 12:00 position to a 10:00 position indicating someone had left through the front door trying to lock it on its way out,

(3) During an electrical storm, our music box would chime though it was never wound as my husband would be reading his book. It just so happens, the objects inside the snow globe music box were that of a little boy and terrier dog.

(4) **UPDATE**: The dog in the snow globe was a terrier. It just so happens that when I spoke to the former owner, her mother had a terrier dog (deceased) that visited frequently and loved to run upstairs and jump onto the right side of the bed. The dog's name was Molly. Strange coincidence? The former owner also reported that one of their cats passed away in the laundry room in 2004. This deceased cat ran across my husband's legs one evening while he was in bed – or at least – from how it was described by the former owner, this was its mannerism.

(5) I would experience hearing and feeling a scratch on my bedspread on top of me followed by a tug of it toward the floor as if an animal had climbed up on the side of the bed and then had attempted to get down grabbing the duvet cover and sheet with it. This event also happened the evening of the electrical storm. **UPDATE**: In speaking to the former owner, her mother's terrier dog had long toe nails that needed trimming. This dog would love to jump up and down from the right side of the bed. By chance could this animal be Molly?

(6) TV turned on by itself in the middle of the night (2:00-2:30 AM) with the remote far from reach and never touched. This happened during a blood full moon.

(7) The children spirits acting playful on occasion and in one situation took my purse neck pouch and hide it under my office chair leaving the neck string hang outside the chair "some" to provide a clue as to how to discover it.

(8) The smoke detectors would go off one after the other when my husband was home alone. Once he changed one battery, another would immediately go off. **UPDATE**: In speaking with the former owner, there was never a time when all smoke detectors needed to

be changed at the same time. Husband felt something strange while this was happening. It just so happens when I returned from my trip (he had been home alone), my clock dials were changed, a sign the children had visited.

(9) It just so happens that the anniversary clock hands were moved a half hour later after the discovery of the purse being found. These events occurred during a full moon. These events occur as a prank or notice that someone has been in the house (a.k.a. children or elderly man).

GHOST APP - KEY TURNED. It was the evening prior to the key being turned in the door that I attempted to make contact with whatever was lurking around in our sitting room causing our dead clock's hands to move. Using my ghost application, the words expressed to me this evening were, "PROPERTY BEHIND UPSET AFRAID." Hearing the word, "AFRAID" would be the 3rd or 4th time. We have no idea who the entity or entities are – perhaps the children or elderly man. **Haunts Continue**: On April 18, 2016, the key was turned to the 1:00 p.m. position. Our TV in our livingroom was "turned off" while we were napping in our chairs. My alarm clock hands were moved to a different position.

QUESTIONS AND THOUGHTS

Is it possible for spirits to communicate feelings and emotions about what happened to them in their former lives? Yes. They may not always demonstrate it but they can lead you to find answers.

Do spirits attempt to find people who they believe will listen to their complaints or protect them from harm? Yes. Seems like my strong-willed soul attracts fearful children or individuals wanting protection. I am not sure how I can protect a deceased spirit other than to tell it to look toward a white light and follow it. If the children were sleeping when they were killed, the idea of their being dead does not resonate with them. One night, while sitting in my office, my husband saw an image of something running from one room to the next. It was a "blur" but he claims he saw something. I suspect it was one of the kids playing hide and seek.

How far should you allow playful activity in your home that may also involve the movement of objects? My answer to this is to set boundaries and not engage in the playful act. First, you have no idea who is "playing" with you. Second, if this involves trickster children (or at least this is what it felt like) ... their wanting attention from you can get out of hand.

Chapter 10
Book Flying Off Shelf

Illustration by Brandy Woods

Chapter 10
Book Flying Off Shelf

PHENOMENA

What is a dirty little secret? Dirty little secrets are often unspeakable truths kept to oneself or by more than one person giving a sense of power, protection, or satisfaction to the person who knows the information most are not privy to. Dirty little secrets are often guarded by those protecting someone, a group, or company image. Dirty little secrets often do not involve respect or loyalty to a particular person, but rather, may be used against people or the company when needed as a form of blackmail. However, what if the dirty little secret isn't about a person, but rather, about something? Namely, a resident ghost.

DEFINITIONS

Agent – a living person who is the focus of poltergeist activity. **Demon** – a negative spirit, purely evil, capable of human possession, possessed of inhuman strength, malevolent, and destructive. **Earthbound** – a ghost or spirit that was unable to cross over to the other side at the time of death and is stuck in this physical plane. **Entity** – anything that has a separate, distinct existence, though not necessarily material in nature. **Feng Shui** - a system of laws considered to govern spatial arrangement and orientation in relation to the flow of energy (qi), and whose favorable or unfavorable effects are taken into account when siting and designing buildings. **Intelligent Haunting** – an interaction on the physical plane as in communication or object movement. **Place-Centered Haunting** – a location where paranormal events frequently take place. **Poltergeist** – a non-human entity (noisy ghost) usually more malicious than ghosts or deceased human beings. May involve thumping, banging, levitation, movement of objects, stone throwing, and starting fires. **Reciprocal Apparition** – a rare type of spiritual phenomenon in which both the agent and the percipient are able to see and respond to each other.

BACKGROUND AND ENCOUNTER

I had worked for several law firms over the years and was good at my job. Each law firm I worked for had its own reputation and character often formed by the variety of personalities who worked for the company. In most of my working situations, although there were many strong personality clashes, what was never tolerated was rude behavior or lack of respect toward another.

My husband worked in a position in a state several hundred miles from where I had been working. I was in need of employment so I applied for a job at a law firm known to have a bad reputation. I was warned to stay out of this law firm as people treated each other rudely, engaged in unfair labor practices, and practiced bully-like behavior against another. I was forewarned that my working for this law firm would bring me regret, stress, hostility, and would be my demise to the unemployment line. I felt my track record with other law firms was solid so I ignored the warnings. I listened but needed a job.

Being perfectionistic, it would be three months until I became a victim of circumstance at the hand of three jealous co-workers and a pushover administrator: The type of jealousy I endured from these three co-workers involved being picked on continuously, blaming me for issues they created, and their attempt to continuously set me up to fail. These moments not only brought me unnecessary stress but continuous anxiety. The pushover administrator had poor listening skills, would take the sides of the jealous co-workers, would put up blinders to hostile situations, and believed the lies spread by my co-workers about me. He had no desire to help me forcing me to play their childish games.

With no one watching my back, it just so happens that while "their game playing" was going on, someone or something was watching their every move made toward me. Namely, it was their dirty little secret, the "resident ghost" of the law firm.

GOT ROCKS? While this backstabbing behavior was going on, I would make periodic visits to my attorney boss' office to leave for him information needed for cases. While in his office, I began noticing that his documents had a single rock placed on top of them giving the impression that they were holding the papers down in place or he was on some Feng Shui movement. Although this seemed like bizarre behavior, I could not tell if he was paranoid about something or warning trespassers about something.

I never asked him what compelled him to place rocks on everything (all over the office) but I began to wonder instead as to why he would be doing so.

RESEARCH. In doing some light research about the building, I did learn that it was believed one or more of the floors were haunted by either former attorneys or individuals who previously worked there. The atmosphere on my floor was exactly as warned to me, uncomfortable and negative.

Eventually, the sense of negativity would get the best of me. I would find that my nervous system could not take the stress any longer. Although my friends advised me to quit, I was not going to leave knowing their tactics were to force me out so I would not be able to obtain unemployment.

BOOK FLYING. One day, when the co-workers had complained up a storm about me (jealousy and witch hunt behavior), the administrator decided to call a meeting to be held in the office of an attorney who would not be there at the time. The general gist of the conversation was that we all needed to learn how to get along with another with a strong emphasis aimed in my direction. Being a victim of their harassment and backstabbing and now being accused of being "the cause", I said nothing and felt like I was living in a nightmare situation.

WATCH OUT. As the meeting adjourned, it was at the point we all stood up and began to leave the room that a book literally "flew" off one of the shelves directly at the administrator missing him by inches. Everyone leaving the room also looked back and gasped with horror. Startled, I turned back and noticed he was looking directly at me as if I had something to do with it. I just gave him a half smile and kept walking.

NO ACCIDENT. The odd behavior of the attorney that I worked for who placed rocks on everything in his office started making sense to me. The atmosphere in his office always felt heavy and unnerving. I can only imagine how often the janitorial staff had been blamed for knocking papers off his desk and onto the floor. I knew as we walked out of that office that the book flying off the shelf directly at the administrator was of no accident. The book was not in a position on the shelf to simply fall off. The room was not shaken. A door was not closed or slammed. The book shelf was not bumped. And, seeing the book "fly off" is different than seeing it "fall off." In my heart, I knew that someone or something was watching my back that day. I believe whoever this entity was attempted to send a message to me that I was not the cause of their problems, but rather, someone to blame and be their punching bag.

TERMINATED. Of no surprise, I was let go from the company two weeks later for "not being a suitable fit." They paid me off with a modest severance check and told me they would not contest my applying for unemployment. What I learned from this situation was that sometimes, "ghosts" can have your back. I knew when that book flew off the shelf that someone was not happy in how I was being treated.

I forgot to thank the ghost who threw the book at them when we left the meeting that day, though I thought about it "in spirit" often.

QUESTIONS AND THOUGHTS

Do I feel there was evil or something demonic haunting that building? Yes and No. How can so many people be affected in such a way where no one was civil to each other? Group think or something more?

After the book flew off the shelf, I knew something resided in that specific office or on that department floor that wasn't quite happy with what they were seeing regarding treatment of another.

Who was haunting the building? I have no idea. I am not sure what the history of the building was prior to the law firm taking possession of some of its floors. All I know is that someone or something from the past was hanging around.

Do I believe the reason why the boss attorney had rocks on his papers was because he believed his office was haunted? I am not sure. For all I know, he was practicing Feng Shui. He didn't appear to be the type who believed in the afterlife, though he behaved like it based on the positioning of the rocks holding his papers down.

Where do you think the hostility came from? Negativity feeds on itself. Negative energies attract and find each other. I'm surprised with all this negativity that I didn't see a full body apparition. Those who feel most comfortable around negativity find company they connect with and feel an alliance to. I never connected with anyone in that law firm, except to the ghost who came to my aid when throwing the book at the administrator and perhaps, my co-workers.

I didn't connect because I didn't have a negative bone in my body and refused to join the unhappy soul group.

Chapter 11
Attacked By A Jealous Woman

Photo by Kelly Renee Schutz

Bed and Breakfast
James Wilkins House, Campbellsburg, Indiana

Chapter 11
Attacked By A Jealous Woman

PHENOMENA

Jealousy can live beyond the grave. On the main floor of this Victorian home, in a large bedroom, lives a resident ghost (female) who makes appearances on occasion to attractive men. Generally, the female ghost likes to remain in the attic. When attractive males stay in the first-floor bedroom, the female ghost makes a visit by wearing perfume, showing affection to them by tugging at their toes, and tucks in their sheets when they sleep in bed. This female ghost, though, does not take kindly to female guests often showing jealousy. As relayed by the owner, the resident ghost, who is friendly to her, called out her name once from behind her when she was walking through the piano room. Upon our departure from this place, the female ghost decided to give a hostile send off.

HISTORY

This elegant Victorian home named the James Wilkins House is located in Campbellsburg, Indiana. The 1894 Queen Anne style home is a true "painted lady" of its time. It echoes with the ambiance of an era long past. In 1999, this home was converted into a bed and breakfast. No further history could be found.[1]

DEFINITIONS

Agent – a living agent who is the focus of poltergeist activity. **Anomaly** – an irregular and unusual event that does not follow a standard rule or law or that cannot be explained by scientific theories. **Apparition** – a rare type of spirit phenomenon in which both the agent and the percipient can see and respond to each other. **Attack** - feeling weak, low energy, dizzy, sick to stomach, ill, and overcome by strong or rotting smells, such as deceased animals or scents. **Ghost** – a form of apparition or supernatural entity visual in appearance of a deceased human spirit. **Chance** – random, unpredictable influences on events. **Contact Session** – period in which paranormal investigators attempt to establish communication with an entity. **Intelligent Haunting** – interaction with an entity on the physical plane, including object movement or touching. **Hallucination** – a vivid perception of sights or sounds that are not physically present; usually associated with an altered state of consciousness. **Illusion** – a perception between what is perceived and what is reality. **Orb** – represents the spirit of a deceased person or animal. Can appear as a ball of light when photographed with differing characteristics such as size, color, density, shape, motion, and flexibility. Origins of cause regarding false orbs can be dust, moisture, insects, or lens reflection. **Reciprocal Possession** – the entry of a spirit into the body of a willing or unwilling host, in which the spirit takes control of the individual's motor and cognitive functions often leading to symptoms of a blackout or hypnotic state of being. **Touched** – the act of having physical contact from a spirit or entity such as pulling hair, shirt tugging, or pushing.

PHOTO 1

Above: Flash bounce on the window frame causing no orb. Seconds later – see below – the same flash bounce with an ORB. My husband smelled perfume during these snapshots. My husband is a skeptic when it involves the paranormal. However, if he feels he is experiencing something unusual – he will bring this to my attention.

PHOTO 2

ENCOUNTER

During a cold weekend in September 2007, my husband and I celebrated my birthday at this bed and breakfast known as the James Wilkins House. While my husband was reading (See Photo 1), he experienced moments of smelling rose water perfume around him. There were no vases with flowers or sachets placed around the room causing this smell. It was at this point I took my camera and started photographing his area asking if a ghost were present to please show itself. I captured an orb (See Photo 2) near the first window. You will note that the flash bounce on the window frame is the same in both pictures. In enlarging the picture, the orb is semi-solid but is not dust or a flash bounce.

TUCKED IN. My husband reported to me the next morning that something "tucked him into bed" the night before by taking his sheet and yanking it gently toward the floor.

ATTACKED. My own encounter with the entity occurred when the owner and I were talking about it as we were "checking out" and saying our goodbyes near our bedroom door. The door made a creaking sound while we were all standing together next to it with no explanation of how the sound was made. No movement of the door occurred, just the sound. The owner looked at the door and addressed the entity in a friendly manner welcoming the ghost into our conversation. It was also at this very moment that I began to feel incredibly tired, dizzy head, and sick to my stomach. These are typical symptoms of a possession and attack. I had to go and sit on the bed because I became so overwhelmed.

WARNING SIGN. The owner put a note on one of the doors in the hallway leading to the 2nd floor telling guests to not go up the stairs to the attic for their own safety. This is where the ghost resided most of the time.

QUESTIONS AND THOUGHTS

Why are women the subject of being attacked in this room? Perhaps the answer lies with the level of jealousy this female ghost has toward them. Can orbs be semi-translucent and be real? Yes. This orb showed up on my print film and its image was imbedded properly onto the film strip. If this orb were dust, it would have first showed up in the first image and then in the 2nd image seconds later. The flash bounce on the window frame is in the same place.

What do you do if you feel you are being attacked? You need to remove yourself from that situation quickly to attempt to release the attacking spirit from your body. You ask the spirit to leave your body and not follow you when you leave. You say, "in Jesus' name, leave my body." My feeling of being attacked by this ghost lasted one mile down the road until I felt as if it left me.

I also noticed and have noticed over the years that I am most vulnerable when I do not feel well (cold, flu, other). In these situations, I do not like to ghost hunt as I feel my weakness or low defenses can make me a target.

Chapter 12
Haunted Marbles

Photo Illustration by Kelly Renee Schutz

Chapter 12
Haunted Marbles

PHENOMENA

SOLD!! How much stuff can a person collect over their lifetime before it becomes a burden of desire? The answer to this question is, "a lot."

If you think about the effort it takes to care for some of our most prized collectibles, you would also not be surprised to learn that as we get attached to some of our objects, we might not be willing to give them up even in death.

AUCTIONS, FLEA MARKETS, GARAGE SALES, SHOPS

Auctions, flea markets, garage sales, and vintage retail shops serve purposes for people. They give people something to do in their spare time. They sell items that can bring us back to moments to reminisce about in our "younger" days. They disperse our collectibles and treasures into the hands of new caretakers. They remind us that nothing can be kept forever. They are places where we can buy, resell, and refurbish items making a profit or loss. Finally, they can bring closure to and lessen the burden on our family members who rid the items cleaning up spaces.

Why is it important that we have connections to our past or to items that provoke our memories?

THURSDAY AUCTIONS

In October 2015, while I was an active vendor at a local craft store, I would find myself in a position where selling my artwork and crafts was not enough to offset my vendor fees each month.

Therefore, the owner of the store encouraged me to attend Thursday night auctions with her to purchase items at low cost and resell in the store tripling the price what we had paid for them. The idea seemed to involve risk but I was willing to expand my marketing strategies to earn the extra cash needed for my vendor fees.

The Thursday auction, run by the German Baptists, intrigued my interest because they offered estate furnishings, vintage items, antiques, and collectibles dating as far back as the 1800's. I knew that people seemed to enjoy purchasing these types of finds.

I, for one, have always liked unusual items … especially items I have never seen before. It is intriguing to have something that the common person does not. The story behind the item can be as interesting and gratifying – provided you know the story.

To me, putting that item among other interesting items, seems to tell a story. I cannot always tell you why I want or need to have something. I cannot always tell you why I yearn to have an item. Could it be the energy it holds that is speaking to me?

BACK IN THE DAY

The objects people collect can tell a story about their lives. At an estate auction, it is humbling to look through box after box and not feel some depression. After all, these items meant something to these people at one time, were cared for and guarded by them in their homes for a long time, were given to them as presents by their loved ones, and, in some cases, had special meaning attached to them. Many of the objects were handed down from generation to generation. In other cases, people who had no one left to pass their things down to were auctioned off or sold at garage sales – down to their baby clothes and high school diplomas and pictures.

When you go into antique or thrift store, it is not uncommon to see pictures or someone's diploma lying among stuff. Do you suppose that person knew when that picture or diploma was achieved that one day ... it would wind up in a junk store with a price tag of $3.00 on it?

How about a portrait of someone who at one time had a name and identity ... hung up on a wall in a restaurant rarely noticed or admired. Some pictures, otherwise known as souls to me, end up in landfills because no one is able or willing to care for it.

HAUNTED OBJECTS

People can become so attached to something that requests are made to be buried with the object at death. This has been practiced for centuries, at least since the time of the Egyptians. Some people have a difficult time letting go of their meaningful possessions and have been known to make special accommodations to be buried in their cars, motorcycles, with their pets, jewelry, etc. not to be shared or given away to anyone. Could it be possible that strong energies attached to some objects can make them haunted?

HAUNTED OBJECTS. There are at least two kinds of haunted objects: (1) objects that absorb energy of their previous owner, and (2) objects that are cursed by a magical ritual, occult, or spell.[1]

According to Ghostly Activities (2016), haunted objects are can be just about anything. The most commonly possessed objects owned with spiritual energy attachment are:[1]
1. Dolls
2. Jewelry
3. Antique bed frames and headboards
4. Paintings (especially self-portraits)
5. Mirrors
6. Clothing (especially gowns)
7. Chairs

Objects that appear to be the most haunted are those that absorb energy. These objects have a great deal of contact with their owner (for example, jewelry), or they capture the image of the owner (for example, mirrors).[1] An untimely death could give the energy to charge the object. For example, a farmer experiences a fatal heart attack and inadvertently charges his clothes and wedding ring with enough essence to become haunted.[1] Before purchasing an item at an auction, estate, flea market, or garage sale, ask about its history before buying it. If needed, you could ask a psychic, one preferably gifted with psychometry, to test the objects before bringing them home.[1] However, if you are not at liberty to have a gifted psychic with you when purchasing at vintage shops, auctions, flea markets, or garage sales, the gamble in what you might bring home is yours. You might also look at your purchases and finds as an adventure in collecting something of interest. After all, there are many fabulous items available to be purchased.

Haunted Object Dormancy and Activity
According to Ghostly Activities (2016), many types of objects remain dormant until there's a change in their environment. Usually, that means a new owner takes the object to a new home, or it is moved into someone else's home. A change in energy, in any respect, can activate an object.[1]

If you have a haunted object, the following ghostly activities may occur:[1]
1. Your possessions may move on their own just from being in the presence of a haunted object.
2. Apparitions and shadow people might manifest.
3. Nightmares become more frequent (3x per week or more).
4. Bad luck happens around the home, including minor injuries or plumbing/electrical problems.
5. Illnesses become more frequent like colds, flu, and food poisoning. People know if experiencing illness and types of illnesses are unusual.

Haunted dormancy and the timing of when it may become activated could coincide with the anniversary of the previous owner's death.

Haunted Object Solutions

According to Ghostly Activities (2016), there are five ways to break the bond with a haunted object.
1. Spiritual cleaning of the object and home.
2. Cleanse the object with salt.
3. Return it to its original place.
4. Bury it in a graveyard.
5. Burn it.

If you are able to set aside what you had invested in your object, then, the best method in ridding its haunted'ness would be to burn or bury it.[1] Otherwise, you could resell it, give it to an unsuspecting friend, or clean it with a salt cleansing solution before doing anything else with it.

Avoid Burning Haunted Objects

According to Ghostly Activities (2016), burning the object should be the very last resort to ridding its haunted'ness.[1] If the object has been burned but continues to show up at your home and you've tried the first 4 object solutions, then seek a paranormal specialist to burn it for you.

For example, on a television show called, *The Haunting*, a gal purchased a framed picture of a man with a cigarette hanging out of his mouth at a garage sale because she was intrigued with it. However, when she had placed the framed picture in her home, she would find the picture moving around to different locations. She also began having nightmares and on occasion, would roll over to find the guy sleeping right next to her. In all cases, she saw "red" in his eyes (sign of the devil). She attempted to take the picture back to its original owner to which the owner shut the door in her face. She tried to throw the framed picture in the trash, only to find it reappearing back in her home. She tried to burn the picture but found the spirit acting out retaliating toward her.

Destroying a haunted object can cause the evil attached to it to 'jump' out. If you haven't mastered protection techniques, it could attach to you or someone who was at the place you burned it. In this case, you will need a pro to destroy the object, break the attachment, and clear your home. Ghostly Activities (2016) has not had to go beyond the 4th solution listed above to "clear" any item.

EXPERIENCES OF HAUNTINGS

How does one known if they have a haunted object in their possession? (1) Most people who experience hauntings say their antique might make them feel cold or anxious. (2) In some cases, the object might give the person dreams or images of times past. (3) Others might claim to have heard voices from the piece, or (4) that it gives off a particular smell. (5) Finally, the item might move on its own.

Regardless, if some types of objects absorb energy, then, the debate about where the hauntings come from remains a mystery. Some experts say that the energy is triggered by neurons firing in the haunted person's brain.[1] Some experts feel hauntings are triggered by something caused by paranormal forces. So, who is right and who is wrong?

ENCOUNTER

One vintage item I like to purchase at auctions is marbles. Marbles have always intrigued me because of their variations in color, their uniqueness, their resistance to deterioration over time as compared to most antiques made out of glass as well as their ability to hold their value.

My fascination with clay marbles, however, takes me to a time period (civil war) I have become intrigued with, namely, the civil war. During the civil war, marbles were played with on a regular basis and eventually used as ammunition for self-protection in wars.

When I bring home marbles from auctions, the first thing I do is to wipe them clean with a rag. In wiping every marble, I feel I am removing unwanted energy and dirt residue left on them from a previous owner who played with them, exposed them to dust, or left them in an aged glass or cigar box sitting on their shelf.

TRANSFER FROM OLD TO NEW. As I began to accumulate marbles, I would transfer each like marble from their respective aged jar to a new jar. They would then be displayed in one or more cabinets in my house.

MARBLE OUTSIDE OF JAR. One day, when I had cleaned a new batch of marbles, I would have a surprise awaiting me. When I opened my curio cabinet door in my sitting room, I would find a lid of one of the jars along with a marble sitting outside of it.

Confused by what I had seen, I asked my husband if he had been looking at them, to which he responded "no." How did the jar lid become undone? How did a marble end up outside of the jar? To date, I cannot answer this question.

It just so happens that the marbles were placed in the same curio unit where the dead anniversary clock sits on a shelf. I spoke about this clock in an earlier story. The dead clock hands would move to different times of the day just before, during or after full moons.

This situation with the marbles only occurred one time but the mystery behind how the lid was undone and a marble was outside the jar remains a mystery. This incident makes me think every time I go to an auction or flea market to find interesting things to buy.

QUESTIONS AND THOUGHTS

Was something trying to get my attention? Did I bring someone home with me attached to an object purchased at an auction? Or, did the marbles attract the ghostly beings that like to play tricks in our house – namely, the ghost children from across the road, the elderly man who makes periodic stopovers, or others?

The important lesson to learn from acquiring "things" is to try and learn something about its origin. If that cannot be answered, then, do a cleaning of the object (if able) to try to remove energy attached to it from those who may have had an attachment to the object.

Chapter 13
Get Off Of My Back

Illustration by Brandy Woods

Chapter 13
Get Off Of My Back

PHENOMENA

More than one ghost haunts the Barcaldine Castle, built between 1591 and 1609, near Oban, Scotland. It is believed Donald Campbell returns to haunt his brother, Sir Duncan Campbell, who was chastised for giving shelter to his murderer. John MacIntosh, a former property manager is said to reside in the Caithness room (tower room) making residual visits to unsuspecting bed and breakfast guests. Some visitors say they have seen the ghost of Donald Campbell, who was murdered at Barcaldine Castle. Others, such as myself, have reported being touched (sat on my back) by John MacIntosh, a residual ghost, in the tower room.

HISTORY OF PROPERTY

Barcaldine Castle, also known as The Black Castle of Benderloch, due to its dark stone used in construction, is a 17th century tower house located 9 miles north of Oban, Scotland. The castle was built by Sir Duncan Campbell, of Glenorchy, between 1591 and 1609.[1] The castle remained in the Campbell family until they fled from it in 1735.[1] The castle was again purchased by the Campbells in 1896 and was restored from disrepair between 1897 and 1911.[1]

John MacIntosh was hired to be the property manager, with family, who all resided in the tower room, known as the Caithness room.¹

As of 2016, this castle is approximately 425 years old.

Photo by Kelly Renee Schutz
The Black Castle of Benderloch, Oban, Scotland
Caithness Room – Tower

DEFINITIONS

Benign Spirit – a spirit that is not harmful. **Chance** – random, unpredictable influences on events. **Haunted Building** – a building, a residence of past or present where paranormal activity tends to be witnessed or experienced by one or more people. **Place-Centered Haunting** – a location where paranormal events frequently take place. **Residual Haunting** – playback of a past event in a continuous loop caused by a trigger or when atmospheric conditions are right. Often associated with past events involving great trauma and tragedy. For example, one might hear someone walking down a hallway, steps, or hear screams at the same time and place as noticed by other witnesses. Researchers believe that some buildings may contain materials that absorb or retain the energy from an event recording it electromagnetically. **Sensitive** - the ability to perceive information through extrasensory perception (ESP). **Sleep paralysis** – a feeling of being conscious but unable to move. **Touched** - the act of having physical contact from a spirit or entity such as hair pulling, shirt tugging, pushing, or sitting on.

SLEEP PARALYSIS

Sleep paralysis occurs when a person passes between the stages of wakefulness and sleep. During these situations, a person may be unable to move or speak for a few seconds up to a few minutes. Some people may also feel pressure or a sense of choking. Sleep paralysis usually occurs either while falling asleep, called hypnagogic or pre-dormital sleep paralysis or when awakening, called hypnopompic or post-dormital sleep paralysis.

THE ENCOUNTER

A heavy feeling that continues to grow stronger awakens you from your sleep giving you a sense that something is sitting on your back. As you awaken, you are conscious enough to move your body but the feeling on your back is getting heavier. Was my experience in the The Black Castle of Benderloch, Caithness room a situation of sleep paralysis? Or, did I encounter the residual ghost of a former property manager who was sitting down somewhere in the room during a normal routine?

AVOIDED THE TOPIC. On May 25, 2015, my husband and I stayed in what was reported to be one of the top 10 haunted castles in Scotland. We chose, as one of our stays, the The Black Castle of Benderloch, also known as the Barcaldine Castle. We stayed in the Caithness room (tower room), which was frequently reported to be haunted. On that day, we arrived late due to a GPS malfunction leading us to a property down the road that certainly did not look like a castle. Upon our arrival, we were greeted by the property owner and given a short tour. I recall asking the property manager if there had been any reported "resident ghosts" in the castle. He didn't say much and basically avoided the topic.

45 STEEP STEPS. Because the journey to our room involved 45 steep steps up a smooth, circular staircase, we decided to go out and have supper at a restaurant a mile down road first before turning in for the evening. Upon our return to the castle, we walked up those 45 smooth steps stopping periodically to catch our breath until we reached the Caithness tower room. As we opened the door to our room, I felt nothing unusual about the environment. I can often tell quickly if we are in the presence of unexplained energy.

As night fell upon us, I found myself needing something from the car, so I begged my husband to go all the way down those steps to retrieve something for me. It was pitch dark outside with no external lights. You know its love when your significant other will go out of a spooky castle, down 45 steep steps, into the pitch dark fumbling his way to find an item in your vehicle. Upon his return, he reported to me that the evening sky was crystal clear, bright stars, shiny moon, and still cool air. I believe the moon phase was nearly full that evening.

It was probably around 11:00 to 11:30 PM when I was testing my ghost equipment, setting out some jingle bells near the bed (used as a ghost alarm) and fumbling with my ghost radar communication application. I had turned on my ghost radar device to see if I could pick up any intelligent words. The first word out of it was "BARK." Moments later, I received a text from my sister back in the

United States informing me that our family dog was killed on the road hours earlier. I was not sure if the word was meant to be sarcastic, so I turned off the device and feeling depressed, went to bed.

I lied on the "right" side of the bed, next to the door leading into the bathroom. From the long drive, rigors of the day, and stair climbing, we were both asleep instantly. It was probably around 2:30-2:45 AM when I awoke to something that felt strange on my back. It was as if a gradual pressure was being applied to my back, like someone was sitting on it. Not ever experiencing this feeling before, I awoke in a panic, wiggled, shook, and thrusted my body in the direction of a wall. The heavy feeling went away. Bewildered, I tried to wake my husband to share the experience. However, as I have seen before in other haunted encounters, it would be difficult to wake him up.

CONFIRMATION. The next morning, I asked the wife of the owner if they ever had a report of what I experienced. She first asked me to describe what happened to me. After I told her, she said, "yes, not often, but the same report – a feeling of something either sitting on a person's stomach or back who lied on the right side of the bed next to the bathroom." I told her if the reports were the same, then, it was likely that what they were encountering was a "residual" ghost.

RESIDUAL GHOST. A residual ghost is not harmful and does not have intelligence. In other words, the ghost had no idea I was lying on the bed when it sat on me. It just went about its routine as it had done so many times before and this was a place where it sat down in that room. A residual ghost experience is comparable to a "playback." It cycles over and over and over. Since the former property manager and his family lived in that room as their main residence, it is possible he was sitting on his bed, sitting in a chair, or sitting by a table.

The fireplace in that room served not only as a stove but was a partial kitchen for his family. Residual playbacks usually occur when there is a trigger or favorable conditions.

NOT THE SAME GHOST. This is NOT the same ghost as reported on the Internet. In fact, little is reported on the Internet about the property manager haunting the Caithness tower room.

QUESTIONS AND THOUGHTS

The one and only question you may ask is "how do I know with certainty that what I experienced was not sleep paralysis?" The answer I will give you is based on these factors: (1) I have never experienced a sensation like this before on my back; (2) I do not waken easily and when I did, I was conscious enough to be able to move my body (whereas in sleep paralysis, reports are people cannot move parts of their bodies); (3) reports that this encounter has happened to others (back or stomach) on the same side of the bed; (4) the fact that the owner's wife asked me for the details first rules out people who are staying in that room believing they had an experience with a ghost. After confirmation of my story, it felt to me as if the ghost was residual and not intelligent (an intelligent ghost is fully aware of what it is doing when interacting with a person); and, (5) this activity had been reported by a number of people over the past five years (not frequently) who stayed in that room with all providing the same details about their experience, sensation, and side of bed.

Chapter 14
Pennies and Pillow Cases

Illustration by Brandy Woods

Chapter 14
Pennies and Pillow Cases

PHENOMENA OF PENNIES

If you look around, you will more than likely see a coin lying somewhere. Pennies and coins are found everywhere - on the ground, on the floor, on countertops, under and in furniture, etc. However, what if a penny drops out of nowhere or is sitting in an unusual spot making the discovery oddly coincidental? Ask yourself this question, "do I believe in signs?"

DEFINITIONS OF SIGNS AND SYMBOLS

Sign - Signs are occurrences that may be informative, mandatory, warning, advisory, or prohibitory. Signs provide us with a sense of meaning about something. For example, when a traffic light turns red, a person knows they must stop. When the traffic light turns yellow, the person knows to slow down anticipating to stop.

Symbol - A symbol is a physical object that has a commonly shared meaning. For example, many people accept the meaning that a cross may symbolize Christianity. People understand when they see a Red Cross that it may symbolize a hospital. Many superstitious people agree that a four-leaf clover may symbolize luck.

PENNY AND PILLOW CASE MYSTERIES

Most people think finding coins is so common that most will not bend over to pick one up or associate meaning to it. If an object is touched or moved at a known location, most people will be puzzled enough to question the mystery behind it.

DEFINITIONS

Anomaly – an irregular or unusual event that does not follow a standard rule or law or that cannot be explained by currently accepted scientific theories. **Apport** – the arrival of an object during a séance or a haunting (animate or inanimate). **Contact Session** – a period of time in which investigators attempt to establish communication with an entity. **Inner Voice** - receiving guidance and assistance from inside of you. **Intelligent Haunting** – an interaction on the physical plane as in communication or object movement. **Spirit Guide** – a spirit who is believed to assist in a person's spiritual journey.

DO GUARDIAN ANGELS EXIST?

Do guardian angels exist? This is a difficult question to answer. My attempt to discover if I had a guardian angel occurred when I was sitting at my computer doing research for this paranormal book. I decided to look up articles on angels on the Internet.

After thumbing through many articles, I found one that caught my eye. In it, the author stated if a person were to go into a meditative state of mind [relax], breath in and out about 20 times, and after the last breath, ask for the name of their guardian angel, that a name would pop into their head or be given a sign that would be visually seen or heard that they had around them, a guardian angel. The article also stated most people felt uncomfortable performing this exercise because the name they felt they heard in their head was caused by their inner voice.

THE ENCOUNTERS

PENNY FOUND. On the day I performed the guardian angel exercise, I had taken a short break from writing and went to my kitchen to grab a quick snack. As I sat at the table and pondered the exercise, I had looked over my shoulder to discover that a penny was lying on the carpet in front of a couch in my livingroom. No one had been sitting in that spot for the past 24 hours. I would consider myself someone who notices everything, so, how did this penny go unnoticed? Did my husband accidentally drop it out of his pocket and simply not notice? When I confronted him, he pled "not guilty."

In reading blogs about people finding pennies, coins, or small objects in places without a reasonable explanation, it appears a widely held common belief about finding objects in an unusual place means a guardian angel or loved is trying to assure the person that they are being watched over or loved.

As I inspected the penny, the only thing I noticed about it was that the date on it said 2001. I tried to think about various meanings and events that may have occurred in the year 2001. Did I have loved ones who may have crossed over during this time? Not that I recall. Was there something symbolic about finding this penny? Not that I could think of. My thoughts remained inconclusive.

PILLOW CASE PULLED BACK. Within an hour after the discovery of this penny, I would go into my bedroom to discover that the case on my pillow had been pulled back exposing half of it. It was not common for my husband or myself to experience our pillowcases slipping off to the point of exposing the bare pillow. Noticing both of these situations within an hour brought confusion and mystery.

This would be the 1st encounter of finding a penny in an unusual and unexplained location and our 2nd encounter in noticing our pillow cases being pulled back or completely removed from the pillows. Was something trying to get our attention?

QUESTIONS AND OBSERVATIONS

Was finding this penny in front of my couch a coincidence? Did my husband accidentally drop this coin in front our couch and not realize it? Or, was something trying to capture my attention giving me a **symbol** of its presence? How do I explain our pillow cases getting pulled back or removed? I am not able to explain either.

Chapter 15
Faces In The Window Screen

Do You See Us?

Photo Illustration by Kelly Renee Schutz
Filtered to Show Ghost People in Window Screen

REAL IMAGE - NOT FAKE

Chapter 15
Faces in the Window Screen

PHENOMENA

My visits to my paternal grandparent's farm as a child and teen were few. On the rare occasion I stayed overnight, my experience in their country home, built around 1905, would provide me with a snapshot of what life may have been like living in that house in a time when few homes had modern facilities. This home had no indoor plumbing or a bathroom.

ORIGINAL HOME. Since the passing of my grandfather and grandmother, the house remained empty with no one to care of it. Although the house has since fallen into disrepair, what remains are remnants of its original architecture and solid construction. This speaks to the exceptional craftsmanship my great grandfather, a farmer and carpenter, had put into the making of that home. This home would eventually pass to his son and then, to my father.

WAS SOMEBODY WATCHING ME? As a sensitive teen, my visits to this home made me feel uncomfortable. Not being familiar enough with the property, there were moments when I had convinced myself that evil surrounded it causing me to avoid the place entirely. I cannot explain why I felt this way. I always blamed that feeling on the way the house looked even though the home was the most "grand structure" of its time and in the county.

GENEAOLOGY. When I was in my early 30's, I made a visit to see my grandmother to discuss the family genealogy. She showed me a picture of a young girl and boy who stood side by side. These children would be the brother (Andrew) and sister (Mary) of my grandfather. Mary passed away around the age of 9-10 years old in my great grandfather's "first home" approximately 2 miles down the road. Andrew lived a full life. Although the young gal in the window screen appears to be Mary, what is interesting to me is that she looks to be 6-7 years old. She has the shape of face and smile as her parents. Her hair appears to be pulled down and back around her head though this was a common hairstyle then. See image that follows. What is also confusing is the man who stands above her. In review of many pictures I have of my great grandfather, what creates confusion is that it appears he did not sport a mustache. The man in the window screen appears to have a mustache. The only other explanation is that it's a deep shadow around his lips. Who is this man?

In seeking the help from an expert psychic, this man is either my great grandfather or is the doctor who cared for Mary on her death bed. I have struggled to verify the identity of this man. See image that follows.

Photo Illustration by Kelly Renee Schutz
Do You See Us Now?

DEFINITIONS

Earthbound – a ghost or spirit unable to cross over to the other side at the time of death and is therefore stuck on earth. **Ghost** – a ghost is believed to be the soul or the life force of a person or animal. **Ghost Hunter** – a person who attempts to gather information of paranormal activity.
Materialization – the formation of a visible physical form of a spirit. **Matrixing – w**hen the mind attempts to manifest images of something they are not.
Manifestation – the appearance or taking of form of an entity. **Skeptic** – to question what others may perceive as real or true.

MY ENCOUNTER

My grandmother passed away a couple of months prior to my taking the picture as seen on the previous page. She left the house vacant and sitting alone. On May 6, 2007, I photographed the ghostly images in the window screen when I made a visit to the property to say goodbye to my grandparents in spirit. It was at this time that I thought this would be my final images and visit to their home. However, little did I realize, I would make several visits back to their home to use my ghost equipment to attempt to make further contact with what showed to me in the window screen or any entity roaming the home and property.

QUESTIONS AND THOUGHTS

Were my suspicions as a teenager confirmed about the property BEING haunted when the images showed in the window? Or, did the property BECOME haunted once my grandparents passed leaving the property empty yet triggering ghostly residents to come back to live in their comfortable home? From what I was told by a ghost expert, the house has a portal underneath its foundation and brings into it all sorts of "unwanted" guests.

THE BRAIN GAME

In 2016, I watched a television show called, "*Brain Games.*" This show demonstrated how the mind is easily fooled and confused when shown images of people's faces "upside down." Most people viewed these images as "right side up" and formed images in their minds that made the images look "human." Because our minds "see" human faces continually, this is why the brain naturally creates images to look "human-like."

If that is true, then, why is it that when the image was shown to about 200 people that they would all DESCRIBE the image with the EXACT SAME details? Or, were their minds playing tricks on them?

YOU BE THE JUDGE. Do you see what appears to be a man, hovering over a young girl in the screened window? Do you see him wearing glasses, his nose, a possible mustache, and his chin? Do you see his eyes? Or, is your brain fooling you by putting these details into the picture?

Although one could argue that the facial details of the man are what men looked like in the 1900's, one cannot simply deny that what you see is oddly real and described the same way in detail by those who see it.

Brain Game? Not all people look alike. What makes this man look unique is that you can actually "see" what appears to be his facial details. Same with the little girl. She appears to be smiling. What is certain though – they are both looking right at me.

ABILITY TO MANIFEST

So, what caused these faces to manifest in the window screen? Most ghosts can only hold their image for about 3-5 seconds. Although most ghosts appear at night (due to mistaken reflections, shadows, and stronger energy fields), ghosts can also appear during the daytime.

It just so happens this manifestation came forth due to a straight-line wind that occurred the morning of my arrival ripping through the property. This storm had knocked over a large tree (away from the house) onto a powerline. With so much electricity still resonating in the air from the storm, you could hear the buzzing sound and feel the electromagnetic waves. It is also believed that a lightning bolt hit the property causing the limestone foundation beneath the home to act as a conductor or absorber for energy. It is also believed these factors combined allowed for the manifestation of the man and young gal in the window.

GHOST HUNTING VISITS CONTINUE

As a paranormal investigator, in order to prove what I photographed in the window that day was real (not mind matrixing), I would need to visit the property several times thereafter to capture more evidence. As a matter of fact, I did capture a moving orb in the basement, a solid orb moving around the livingroom, had my camera batteries die in the barn, and was surrounded by hundreds of orbs when standing on the front steps of the home on a full moon evening. All situations where I captured evidence occurred during a storm or moon phase.

DAY TRIP IN 2017

My sister and I always liked to ghost hunt on the property (house and barn). There was a day (afternoon) mid-2017 (cannot recall if March or later), when we decided to go to the property to ghost hunt. With the house falling apart and black mold taking over the kitchen ceiling, it was important to bring masks to not breathe in black mold spreading all over the house. Our intent was to not stay in the house very long. Of course, we forgot to bring masks.

Battling tall weeds and grass to get to the falling apart house was always a challenge. During the earlier months, several wood ticks would cling to a person just walking a short path to the front door of the house. This was one way to keep unwanted visitors from going over there.

As we approached the house, we noticed the hole (outside porch leading into the house) was getting bigger. This small area was just enough to detain a person from entering with ease. A risk for anyone who didn't understand that stepping into that hole would result in falling 5' feet downward onto a dirt covered basement while cutting up their legs (rotting wood).

As we entered the door that led into the kitchen, my sister and I noticed the black mold on the ceiling spreading. It looked as if its mission were to take over the entire place. I do not believe we went upstairs that day although it was in as bad as shape as the downstairs. The narrow steps that led upstairs were always covered with white dry wall pieces ... making the journey to reach the top even more difficult and risky.

The house and property had no electricity. It did have, though, copper wiring in its walls. The rooms (diningroom, livingroom, adjacent porch, and upstairs) were all rotting from the inside out. The pink (or were they green) curtains still hung in their places (diningroom and livingroom) as if they were forgotten. A small candle, never burned, still sat on the ledge in a window in the livingroom. Cannot recall if the pink hand-held dial phone on the wall remained.

Mice that didn't survive the winter lie flattened (decomposed) on the diningroom floor among a lot of ceiling tile debris and insulation. The walls in the livingroom, covered with a wet runny mold stain from top to bottom, remind us that deterioration occurs over time.

The sewing area (a nook) was completely rotted out. The narrow porch, attached to the home, was falling off. The place was and still is, as of this writing, a deterioration mess. Despite all of this, the ghosts do not seem to mind the look of the deteriorated environment and gather there for whatever reason.

With K-2 meter in hand (sweatshirts over our noses), my sister and I proceeded to walk into the kitchen area. As we stood and stared at its condition, we began visualizing how it was set up back in the day. After all, two generations lived in this house.

It would later be discovered that much of the furniture that remained in that house was handed-down from my great grandfather to grandfather to father. Much of it now in the hands of my generation, the great grandchildren.

As my sister and I stood in the kitchen, we began asking questions to attempt to make contact. Regardless of the moon phase that day (clear afternoon), we were successful. But with "whom" did we make contact?

The house and barn seem to be haunted every time we go over there. My ghost application device spit out the words "UPON … EVERYONE." I took that to mean that we stumbled upon a group gathering. Distracted for just a second, as we looked away, my K-2 meter then zipped to 5 bubbles (we saw it). It was at this point that I felt breathless and needed to get out of the house. I didn't know if it was because I was being affected by the black mold or the lack of oxygen while breathing underneath my sweatshirt.

As we were leaving, I felt like I was going to pass out. My sister walked ahead of me. I instructed her to keep an eye on me because I couldn't breathe very well. The sense I had was that something was wrapped around me. I then felt attachments all over me. But who was attaching? And, of course ... why?

As I entered my car, I kept shaking myself in all directions telling whomever to get off me and go back to the house. As I turned the car on, I needed to continue my plea with a stern voice. The feeling subsided about a mile down the road.

Since my father passed away in December 2016, I have not been able to go back inside this house alone. However, I would sit in my car at the end of the driveway and look at a property that was once in its glory days ... now a deteriorated mess. Let me not forget to mention ... also a property haunted by ghosts (former residents and strangers).

Chapter 16
Haunted Classroom

Illustration by Brandy Woods

Chapter 16
Haunted Classroom

PHENOMENA AND HISTORY

Below is an image taken in 1929 of the Ross National Sanatorium, located in what was referred to then as rural Dayton, Indiana. The location, as of 2016, is within the city limits of Lafayette, Indiana. As of 2016, the Ross Building is the administration building located on the Ivy Tech Community College campus.

Photo Courtesy of Allen County Public Library
Ross Building, Lafayette, Indiana

HISTORY. A **sanatorium** (also spelled **sanitorium**) is a medical facility for long-term illness, most typically associated with treatment of tuberculosis (TB) before antibiotics. Back in the 1920's and early 1930's, this building was used to treat people who contracted tuberculosis (TB). Several people died from having this disease in this building although the actual number is unknown. One person was known to have passed away in this building on December 23, 1929. Others, suspected of having TB, were treated in this building. In review of a blog on the Internet, it made mention that someone's mother went here as a little girl in the late 1920s or early 1930s. She and other classmates had TB tests at school and tested a false positive. They would go here to get a chest x-ray.

HAUNTINGS IN THE ROSS BUILDING

I do not have much to report about the hauntings in the Ross building. All that I know is some hauntings occur either in the basement or attic of this building. Those who currently work in this building disclose little to nothing about their encounters. These hauntings do not remain exclusive to this building. Some of apparitions have made their way out of the Ross building and into a building across the lawn from it. A few years after I began teaching on this campus, I had unexplainable experiences in my classrooms.

DEFINITIONS

Agent – a living person who is the focus of poltergeist activity. **Authentication** – proving genuine verification of facts surrounding an occurrence of paranormal phenomena. **Chance** – random, unpredictable influences on events. **Clairaudience** – auditory form of ESP paranormal information received outside the range of normal perception through voices, whispers, and auditory impressions. **Earthbound** – a ghost or spirit that is unable to cross over at the time of death. **Intelligent Haunting** – an interaction on the physical plane as in communication or object movement from a spirit who is conscious. **Place-Centered Haunting** – a location where paranormal events frequently take place. **Poltergeist** – non-human entity (noisy ghost) usually more malicious or destructive than ghosts or deceased human beings. May involve thumping, banging, levitation or movement of objects, stone throwing, and starting fires. **Touched** – the act of having physical contact from a spirit or entity such as pulling hair, shirt tugging, pushing, tapping on shoulders and backs, etc.

HAUNTINGS COME TO ME

I began teaching on the Ivy Tech Community College campus in 2004. I was not aware then that the campus had a history of disease and death (TB). Although this would not have changed my decision about working there, what it did do was authenticate my encounters. Even though my ghost hunting investigation did not begin in full swing until 2007, I was still quite naïve and oblivious to anything "odd" happening around me in my classrooms.

MY ENCOUNTERS

CIVIL WAR HAT. My perception about the campus environment began to change around 2007. My boss and I would share ghost stories with each other once he learned that I was enthusiastic about staying at haunted properties while on vacation. It would be days after I returned from a trip to Myrtles Plantation in Louisiana that he would call me into his office and ask me if I "brought back" someone with me because his "civil war" hat that was located on a high shelf in his home office was sitting on a chair when he got home from work one day.

This had scared him to death (figuratively). He was so panic'ed by this that he thought someone was spying on him in his home. I told him that it was possible that I unknowingly brought someone back with me (attachment) which made him feel somewhat relieved but anxious.

VOICES. My first classroom paranormal encounter with one or more resident ghost(s) took place around 2009. I was teaching in my usual classroom relaying an assignment to my students when I made a specific request for no talking or interaction with one another during a movie clip. As I began playing the movie clip, I had overheard what sounded like a lot of chatter coming from the back of the room. The room was very dark at the time. Annoyed by this, I stood up and was about to wave my hand at the two boys in the back asking them to not talk when I realized they were not only sitting far apart from each other but were both focused on doing the assignment. I sat back down in my chair and began to wonder if I was losing my mind. Within the month, I would ask my boss if he had any knowledge of the history of the campus. He had told me it had once been a sanitarium for ill people and that several deaths occurred in the building across from our building. I thought to myself, "why are these ghostly apparitions coming to me?"

WHISPERING. I never shared my experiences I had in my classrooms with anyone for fear of looking like a crazy person. Although I thought my experiences were few, it would be that next semester when I would realize the encounters would become more aggressive in wanting attention from me. It was during a break when one student, who was sitting against the wall, looked at me and said, "I know you are going to think I am crazy, but I am hearing voices in this classroom." My response was, "oh, what kind of voices?" "Whispers." "Oh." "I know you must think I am nuts." "No, I don't think you are nuts." "Do you believe in ghosts?" "Well, I didn't think I did but I have no idea where these voices are coming from." It was at this point that I told the student that if there were ghosts in the room that they were not to be feared. So ... I thought.

TAUNTED. Moving into the next semester, a student of mine was sitting in the middle of the aisle "jerking" and "twitching" all the time. During a break, I asked her if she was feeling okay.

The student looked at me and said, "you are going to think I am a nut case but I think I am being harassed by a ghost." [Me] "Why would you think that?" [Student] "Because I live in a house with a ghost and I think it followed me here and it won't stop tapping me on my shoulder." [Me] "Oh, why would it be doing that?" [Student] "To taunt me." She proceeded to tell me about her living situation where she would watch a broom stick being thrown down the stairs (by itself), her possessions thrown all over the place (in front of her), the cat would stare in a particular area (with no explanation), and she was a wreck with stomach issues.

PROJECTOR. Soon after this incident, a few more reports would come in from students telling me that they were feeling uneasy sitting in the back of my classroom (hearing voices). Next, I would start experiencing video equipment failures (continuously) in that room.

There were even times when I asked the "ghosts" to leave my equipment alone since I needed to stay on schedule for class.

To demonstrate how out of control it got, I was teaching in the room next door one semester and my video projector started blinking and acting up. To make light of the situation (to not alarm the students), I looked up at the projector and said, "now stop that" ... to which the projector responded back to me immediately with the sound and flash of "blink-blink" ... you could hear a pin drop. I couldn't hide the "secret" any longer. The fear on my student's faces when that happened was almost too much to bear. I told them about the history of the property and to not be afraid.

DANGER. I was teaching on another campus (same college – different location) several miles away. The town was known to have a lot of paranormal activity. Knowing I attract ghosts from every corner of the universe (so it felt to me), I didn't feel as if I was in much danger at this location.

HEAD HITS WALL. The building I taught was a former newspaper printing office. People felt uneasy going down into the basement. One day, as I was getting myself prepared for class, when I went to sit down in my chair, it felt like something had pulled it out from underneath me causing me to fall backwards hitting my head against the wall (small concussion), and chair busting a hole right through the wall. Was this an accident? Or was this the work of something evil?

INJURIES and FIRE. Embarrassed, I got up off the floor to save face and pretended I was fine. I wasn't fine. Within the week, a computer would fall on one of my student's legs in the next room. A door handle (same room) would fall off when pulled to shut the door, nearly locking all of us into that room with no alternative escape. A "smoke" smell would show up continuously and fester near my computer with the fire department being called nearly 10-15 times that month to check out every corner of the building to find the cause. Inconclusive. Coincidence?

QUESTIONS AND THOUGHTS

Where did these apparitions come from and why did they need so much attention from me? Apparitions that taunt a person are not necessarily evil. Apparitions that cause injury and create fire smells are evil.

Chapter 17
Dance Manifests Music

Illustration by Brandy Woods

Chapter 17
Dance Manifests Music

PHENOMENA

(Niece Twirling) … "What was that?!!" A reaction I will never forget when my 9-year old niece was dancing playfully in her livingroom one clear, late afternoon. Out of nowhere, we had both heard music manifest in the middle of her livingroom floor. The music played for about 5 seconds as she twirled around and sang. And then, the music suddenly stopped when she reacted. That event was so unusual that even I, lying on the couch, was alarmed by it. Where did this music come from?

WHAT WE KNOW

We know it is possible for sound to travel long distances often carried by the wind or in very cold conditions. For example, when the air current is just right, my relatives were able to hear a telephone ringing inside a restaurant that was located nearly 3 miles away.

However, what if this sound was so unusual that there simply was no explanation for it? The home was sound proofed with the windows and doors closed that day. This incident would not only raise questions but would nag me enough to start asking questions about what my niece's home was built on. Did she and her parents live on sacred Indian burial grounds? Did they encounter other unusual experiences they assumed were nothing more than mere coincidences? Have the pets been reacting to anything odd?

DEFINTIONS

Agent – a living person who is the focus of poltergeist activity. **Chance** – random, unpredictable influences on events. **Clairaudience** – an auditory form of extra sensory perception (ESP) in which paranormal information is received outside the range of normal perception through voices, whispers, and auditory impressions. **Earthbound** – a ghost or spirit that is unable to cross over at the time of death. **Intelligent Haunting** – an interaction on the physical plane as in communication or object movement from a spirit who is conscious. **Place-Centered Haunting** – a location where paranormal events frequently take place. **Skeptic** – to question what others may perceive as real or true. **Sound** – a vibration that travels through the air or another medium and can be heard when it reaches a person's or animal's ear.

HISTORY OF INDIAN BURIAL GROUNDS

According to Mary Jane Smetanka (October 4, 2014), news reporter, who wrote an article for the *Star Tribune*, state of Minnesota, about sacred Indian burial grounds, many development projects have been halted because Indian burial sites are protected and must not be disturbed.[1]

With more than 12,500 mounds scattered across Minnesota, they are especially common in Bloomington, Eden Prairie, Red Wing, Shakopee, Prior Lake, Savage, and around Lake Minnetonka. Mound, formerly known as Mound City, was named for the bumps and rises that marked Indiana burial grounds.

According to Smetanka (2014), in Minnesota, it is a felony to "willfully disturb" a burial ground. The issue about disturbing a burial ground continues to cause conflict such that the Dakota and Ojibwe Indians, who once lived in these areas, honored their dead by burying them in the best locations they could find such as high, dry spots, often in areas offering beautiful views of lakes and rivers.

In some places, such as Mound, Minnesota, houses built during the past century, many of them in the 1880's, were constructed on top of these sacred burial mounds. Some residents, unable to build onto their homes due to a "mound" situated in their backyards, stated the lack of disclosure from their title companies resulted in lawsuits.

While lawsuits are not common, clashes between development and burial sites consume much time to authenticate unplatted areas more than 50 years old. "If there is a grave on the property, nothing can be done," according to Scott Anfinson, Minnesota State Archaeologist. Often, a final decision about development projects is made by the Indian Affairs Council.

Up until the 1970's, people acted as they wished in removing or moving the mounds. In the early 1900's, tourists visiting resorts and hotels would take their pick and spades to dig for treasures. Science digs ended around 1974.

In the 1880's, about 524 mounds were mapped at 48 sites near Lake Minnetonka. It had been reported in the years 2014-2016 that of the 524 mounds originally mapped, only 40 remained at 12 sites.

QUESTIONS AND OBSERVATIONS

Is it possible for the souls of buried native Indians to reach out from the grave to rejoice in dance? Was this residual music triggered from something of past? The music lasted 5 seconds and stopped. It never manifested again after that moment. Weather conditions were perfectly clear and calm. Doors and windows were closed during the incident sound proofing the home.

The family lived in a townhome on Indian land. They have never reported hearing drifting noises from their neighbor's homes. The music that played was not a tune that either my niece or I recognized. No music boxes were lying around. No sound applications played from a cell phone. Inconclusive.

Chapter 18
Visitors in the Barn

Photo Illustration by Kelly Renee Schutz
Century Barn

Chapter 18
Visitors in the Barn

PHENOMENA

"When things go bump -- I mean – when things get moved around in the barn." It was around April 2011 when I was having a discussion with my ghost psychic about several of my unexplained experiences. During the middle of our conversation, she asked me if I had any plans to ghost hunt in my grandparent's barn, and if not, to consider doing so because it had "occupants." Of course, with hesitation, I said, "why would I do that?" I didn't give her suggestion much thought until a month later when I had changed my mind.

As an investigator enthusiast, one should never "ghost hunt" alone. This can be dangerous for a variety of reasons. Most of you might think ghost hunters are fearless and are not afraid of unknown places. Well, the truth be known, most of us are not sure what hazards we might encounter. This may include other conditions such as molds, toxins in buildings, at risk pavements, crumbling foundations, open wells, holes in the ground, stray animals, and boards/materials with loose or rusty nails. And, of course, friendly or not so friendly, "ghosts."

I didn't want to go into that barn alone but my curiosity got the best of me. So, I did what most big sisters do -- I invited my younger brother and sister to go along with me. SOMEONE had to be there to save me. It was on this cold, rainy, damp day, we gathered up our gear, said a prayer for protection, and with ghost hunting equipment in hand, we proceeded to go INSIDE the barn.

DEFINITIONS

Agent – a living person who is the focus of poltergeist activity. **Attacked** – a form of physical or emotional distress caused onto the target person, such as hurting the person physically (scratches, bruises), making person physically ill, causing a sense of being dazed or dizzy. **Collective Apparition** – a rare type of sighting in which more than one person sees the same apparition or phenomena. **Contact Session** – a period of time in which paranormal investigators attempt to establish communication with an entity. **Ghost Hunt** – a carefully controlled project in which various methods and equipment used to investigate reports of ghosts and hauntings. **Illusion** – a perception between what is perceived and what is reality. **Intelligent Haunting** – an interaction on the physical plane as in communication or object movement from a spirit who is conscious.

Poltergeist – a non-human entity (noisy ghost) usually more malicious or destructive than ghosts or deceased human beings. May involve thumping, banging, levitation or movement of objects, stone throwing, and starting fires.
Touched – the act of having physical contact from a spirit or entity such as pulling hair, shirt tugging, and pushing.

<u>TRIGGERING THE ENCOUNTER</u>
I suppose you could say that I was to blame for starting the disturbance that went on between myself and the "ghostly occupants" who resided in the barn.

DETAILS. When my brother and I arrived onto the property, for some reason, I began feeling overly nervous about going into that barn. After all, if my expert ghost psychic says it was haunted, then, it must be haunted. I had worked myself up so much that I caused myself to have stomach issues. And, when I have stomach issues, I need a restroom. And, guess what, the place had NO restroom except for a broken down outhouse that was located about a 100-yards away from the barn in overgrown weeds. And, I wasn't going to go into THAT outhouse even if it were the last place on earth. As I tried to calm myself down, my stomach pains grew worse. Was I causing my stomach pains or something else?

UNLATCHING THE DOOR. As my brother unlatched the door to the barn, I could feel my heart racing and stomach gurgling. As we walked inside the barn, all I heard was "dead silence." If you ever find yourself in a place where it sounds "dead silent" ... chances are likely, YOU ARE NOT ALONE.

NEED FOR RELIEF. At that point, my brother was on a discovery mission and I was on a mission to find a spot to relieve myself. As my stomach pains grew more intense, I couldn't tell if I was being attacked by something or if my nerves were getting the best of me. As gross as this may sound, imagine being somewhere where you can't go to the bathroom but need to badly. It was at this point that I asked my brother to leave the barn because my grunting would have distracted him from his mission to find a ghost. I found a pile of HAY on the floor near the wall. And, you guessed it ... down the pants went. However, I think this was the very moment I violated something precious to the ghostly occupants in that barn because the barn environment suddenly changed from calm to intense.

My brother came back inside the barn. My sister arrived on the scene and entered with him. We all stood inside the door attempting to make contact with the occupants.

While venturing in the barn, my brother found a vintage powder container (see image next page) and placed it on the ledge of a cement feed trough (where cows ate). Soon after he did this, we all heard what sounded like a

ROCK being thrown against something in the corner of the barn. As we looked at each other in confusion, my brother noticed that the powder container that he placed on the cement ledge was now in a different spot other than where he put it moments prior. It was at this point that I asked my sister to start snapping pictures (with me) in a general area with her camera. No sooner than we tried to shoot an image together, SPARKS flew out of both of our cameras and our new batteries went DEAD. It was at this point that my gut feeling about violating the hay and being in there snooping around was perhaps what upset "the ghostly occupants" in there, so, we took the hint, apologized, and left.

Photo by Kelly Renee Schutz

QUESTIONS / THOUGHTS

Did I trigger "something" when I violated a hay pile possibly offending one or more of the ghostly occupants in the barn? It should be noted that weather conditions felt right for this haunting (rainy, wet, bitterly cold). My ghost expert psychic described the ghostly person watching us in the barn to be that of an older woman with long black hair that caused our camera batteries to go dead once we attempted to take pictures. I presume she was talking about my great grandmother. My psychic described the other occupant in the barn to be someone dressed in uniform (army) that didn't grow up on the property who sought refuge there for privacy.

Chapter 19
"Silent Night, Holy Butterfly"

Illustration by Brandy Woods

Chapter 19
"Silent Night, Holy Butterfly"

PHENOMENA

Losing a loved one can be devastating and life changing. Losing both parents two years apart can cause reactions of disbelief. When we grieve the loss of a loved one, some of us may look for "signs" or "symbols" to assure us that our loved ones remain near, even if on a temporary basis. Our perceived observances of signs and symbols often aid in our healing lessening the effects of grief.

My husband's parents passed away two years apart. Both shared a strong Catholic faith. Both loved their children deeply. With their passing, there was no doubt in anyone's minds that their being spiritual brought them to heaven. However, even though my husband believed his parents had passed to a better place, he could not help but notice a few indicators that made him rethink the possibility of that they may have been contacting him after death.

Two signs and one symbol showed to my husband after each passing. These situations were so unusual that he questioned the idea that the spirit of someone CAN exist after death. Three situations occurred: (1) with his father's passing, the noticing of a butterfly on a bitterly cold winter day, (2) at his father's funeral, a light that blinked on and off during the eulogy, and (3) when his mother passed, my hearing "Silent Night, Holy Night" outside in the car lot in the middle of October with no known music source.

DEFINTIONS

Agent – a living person who is the focus of paranormal activity. **Clairaudience** – an auditory form of ESP, paranormal information is received outside the range of normal perception through voices, whispers, and auditory impressions. **Hallucination** – a vivid perception of sights and sounds not physically present (associated with altered state of consciousness). **Intuition** – a non-paranormal knowledge gained through perceptive insight. **Sign** – a sign can be the meaning we interpret from something that is informative, mandatory, warning, advisory, or prohibitory in nature. **Symbol** - a symbol is a physical object that stands for something such as, a cross may symbolize Christianity; a black cat crossing in front of you may symbolize the onset of bad luck. **White Noise** – an acoustical or electrical noise of which the intensity is the same at all frequencies within a given band.

ENCOUNTER WITH FATHER

My husband was very close to his father. His father passed away late November 2011, just shy of Thanksgiving. Having a terminal illness with prognosis of

3 weeks to 3 months, he survived 6 months. My husband and I lived 650 miles away in another state. Our living this far away posed many challenges when trying to make visits. *Time of someone's passing is not determined by how far we live away.*

When we received notice that his father's condition was grim, we set out driving from our home during the late evening hours (9 of 12 hours) before we stopped for the evening. Getting an airfare ticket was not an option. With 3 hours to drive the very next day, we felt we were going to make it before his father passed away. Unfortunately, at the point of our waking up in the morning, the phone call came in that he passed. My husband would not have his opportunity to say goodbye to his father.

Time of someone's passing is not determined by our schedules. My husband was devastated in not being given a final moment to say goodbye to his father.

"SIGN" AT FATHER'S FUNERAL

My husband and I are both believers in "unusual signs." Not all signs capture our attention, just those that appear to be oddly coincidental.

FUNERAL. During his father's funeral, as I was sitting in the front row listening to the Pastor give the eulogy, I began to think about why his father didn't wait for my husband to see him one last time before he passed. Why couldn't his father have just held on a little longer knowing his son was doing everything in his power to get to him? *Time of someone's passing is not determined by our schedules.*

LAMP. As the Pastor was giving the eulogy, I couldn't help but notice a tall lamp in the front corner of the room near some flowers. The lamp started to blink "on and off, on and off." The light movement was not a quick electrical flicker but a very smooth "on and off" blink. I had seen this type of blink before when we stayed at a bed and breakfast in Pennsylvania near a cemetery where our lamp in our bedroom started blinking for no reason. Being a ghost investigator, I immediately started asking questions to determine if a haunting was occurring in that room. How I knew the situation to be real was I had asked questions and it blinked in response to my questions. Therefore, I took this similar "blinking" motion to be a sign from someone, believed to be his father.

After the service, I approached one of the people who worked at the funeral home and asked him if he ever encountered the lamp blinking before (other funerals or in general). He said, "not generally." He then told me about a man who lived upstairs in the building who was discovered dead in his apartment. He was not sure if the man died of natural causes or suicide. He also told me the light bulb was brand new and that they didn't have electrical issues in the building. My gut feeling was that it was not the man upstairs but rather, his father sending a sign of his presence. Those of us who are spiritual may want to believe that signs presented to us are real AND not the result of a coincidence.

SYMBOLS. Many people believe butterflies to be a visual symbol that provides confirmation or a message from a guardian angel or loved one that all is peaceful. Just after a person passes, symbols such as a butterfly, bird, or pigeon are often noticed and accepted as being a sign from a loved one. Symbols can often show up in places not typical of their being noticed with no logical explanation as to how they got there. Regardless, symbols are meaningful to people and commonly accepted as a message relayed from a loved one or angel.

BUTTERFLY IN DOORWAY. Adjusting to the change of having a loved one leave our physical plane can take some time to process. Remaining focused during our healing process can have its struggles.

My husband's father passed away just before Thanksgiving. On Thanksgiving day, the immediate family celebrated a meal in the nursing home conference room, just steps from where his father resided on his final days.

On this Thanksgiving day, the weather outside was bitterly cold but offered in return, a bright, sunny day. Just after lunch, we all decided to go back to the assisted living apartment to visit with the mother. As we walked through the dining hall, a place where his father ate regularly, we approached a doorway that led to a long hallway that we all needed to walk through. As each of us passed through the doorway, we noticed a Monarch butterfly sitting on the floor in the doorway spreading its wings calmly back and forth.

The nursing home did not have a butterfly exhibit for its residents. Monarch butterflies do not survive winter months in this state.

Residents were not allowed to have cages with butterflies in them. No one was allowed to bring them in. No one reached down to touch the butterfly as we walked by as we felt it was not proper.

QUESTIONS / THOUGHTS

Where did this butterfly come from? How was this butterfly able to survive a bitterly cold winter month?

Never seeing them in the building before, was this butterfly meant to be a **symbol** or mere coincidence? Some of the family members believed the butterfly to be that of a guardian angel while others believed it to be the father.

"SIGN" AT MOTHER'S PASSING

My husband's mother passed away nearly two years later. During the middle of October 2013, unlike his father, my husband was able to spend nearly a week with his mother. Unfortunately, like his father, he would not be able to be by her side during her final moments. *Time of someone's passing is not determined by our schedules.*

It was a very beautiful Fall day. The leaves were golden yellow, the sun was shining, and the birds were chirping. A light breeze rustled the trees. We (his brother, sister-in-law, husband, me) all took turns being by his mother's side the morning and early afternoon before she passed.

It was around mid-morning that same day when my husband and I needed to travel out of state for an event and then, return to our jobs. His mother's condition when we left her was grim but showed no change as compared to other days. We left telling her we would return within the week. *Time of someone's passing is not determined by our schedules.*

My husband and I had driven about 4 hours out of state when he received "the call" that she had passed. With my husband driving the vehicle upon this notification, you can only imagine how helpless I felt sitting in the passenger seat with him in a distraught condition. My challenge was to have him pull off the road to collect his emotions, thoughts, and grieve. When we left her four hours prior, her condition didn't show much of a change. Her passing came suddenly, unexpectedly, and not as anticipated.

ENCOUNTER WITH MOTHER?

We did not turn around to go back as his brother had everything under control. We checked into our hotel. When we walked into our hotel room, nothing felt out of the unordinary. With both of us in a daze from hearing the news about his mother passing, I needed to distract myself further by going out to our car to get something.

MUSIC. On my way out of the hotel, I felt light headed, dizzy, and sick to my stomach. These are typical symptoms of shock or my having a paranormal encounter. While walking over to our car, I noticed my ear drums starting to pinch with my hearing the music, "*Silent Night, Holy Night.*" As the pain intensified in both of my ears, I noticed the music kept on playing over and over. I stopped to look around me to see if there was any logical explanation as to where the music was coming from. After all, it was the middle of October and this music seemed unusual for this time of year.

Looking around, I saw in front of me a building with all windows closed. To the left of me, a busy highway with lots of car noise. To the right of me, a church (ah hah – a church with a bell tower). However, the noise didn't appear to be coming from that church. My ear drums hurt so bad that I needed to hold my hands over them. I grabbed my things from the car and headed back inside.

ODD COINCIDENCE? When I entered our room. I told my husband to go out to our car and tell me what he could hear playing in the parking lot. He went outside and when he came back he said, "what exactly was I listening for?" He heard nothing. Either the music stopped playing or there was never any music to hear to begin with. All I know is WHAT I heard was odd for the time of year and hurt both of my ear drums forcing me to put my hands over them.

MOTHER'S FAVORITE SONG. I told him that what was playing was, "*Silent Night, Holy Night*" and that it continued over and over not stopping. To which he said to me, "that was my mother's favorite song." My gut feeling then recalled the pinching in my ear drums (piercing) as well as my inability to locate where the sound was coming from. My belief was that this was a sign from his mother trying to make contact with me to assure "him" that she was okay. I took this moment as an opportunity to relay to him that his mother was near him and that she made it to heaven and was alright. Sound crazy? Keep reading.

In relaying this moment to my ghost expert psychic, she told me that souls do not often part quickly when they die. That souls can linger on earth for hours until they are ready to go to the next astral plane. For some reason, I have a tendency to believe that energy can linger not always "crossing over" upon death.

Assumptions about when a person might die can often play tricks on us because even though people appear to be getting better, often it is a sign that they are within their last moments on this earth. *Time of someone's passing is not determined by our schedules.*

DRAWER IN ROOM. One could also argue that when I felt dizzy that I was experiencing shock or trauma. In this same hotel room, on my way to the shower, I noticed a drawer next to my side of the bed was pulled out. I asked my husband if he had been looking for a Bible. He said, "no." This drawer being open could have gone unnoticed when we entered the room or was an additional sign.

What I know to be true with my paranormal encounters is that when one unusual event occurs, something else will follow making the "coincidence" of the first incident something I can validate.

QUESTIONS AND THOUGHTS

Was the dresser drawer open when we arrived into the room but didn't notice? Was the music heard in the parking lot a mere coincidence? Where did the music come from? How far can sound travel on windy days where it can hurt your ears?

COUPLE VALIDATES CAR LOT MOMENT

FOLLOW-UP. About a year or two later, I was riding on a shuttle bus back to a hotel to pick up my car. Next to me, was a couple who lived in the area near that hotel where we stayed the day of his mother's passing. This couple went to the church that was right next door to that hotel that had a bell tower. Here was my opportunity to ask some questions: (1) How active are you in your church? "Very." (2) Does that church play music from the bell tower? "No, it's been broken for years and too expensive to fix." Are there Christmas rehearsals in October? "No." Do you know of any other place in the area that plays music so loudly that it carries all the way to your church and parking lot? "Not that we are aware of." My conclusion to all of this was that I encountered a "sign."

Chapter 20
Orbs Relaying Messages

Photo by Kelly Renee Schutz
Image Taken March 2015 (Blood Moon)

There are at least 4 REAL ORBS in this picture (see arrows). The colors of the solid orbs are cream, gray, white, and blue. When this picture was taken, I felt nothing near me. I stood in "dead silence" on the porch steps by my grandparent's house looking out into a clear sky. I always knew I could attract a ghostly crowd. Who or what are these entities?

Chapter 20
Orbs Relaying Messages

PHENOMENA

Whether it be print film or a digital camera, orbs frequently show up in pictures. Orbs generally take the appearance of being a round circle with a solid or translucent mass. Orbs are considered "balls of energy." Orbs confuse people as to what they are. Some people feel capturing an orb is the same as capturing an entity or spirit that is either human or animal. The phenomena of orbs sparked a lot of controversial conversation several years ago and continues to be a debated topic by investigators and non-believers alike. "What are they?" "Who are they?"

DIGITAL VERSUS PRINT FILM

Prior to the development of digital cameras, people were capturing orbs on their print film images but discounting them as being a defect. They also viewed orbs as a nuisance intrusive to their photo efforts. It was when the first digital cameras came into widespread use that people began paying attention to the "round circles with masses" while questioning whether digital imagery had begun to capture more than what one could see with the naked eye. People who are sensitive or have strong beliefs in the afterlife generally believe that capturing an orb on their picture is either a sign of paranormal activity or that a loved one has made its presence.

FALSE ORBS

False orbs (still or in motion) occur in video and pictures all the time. Professional photographers like me are less likely to capture an orb with my equipment if my lens has a UV coating on it. A UV coating filter can block orbs from showing in our pictures. This can also explain why some people capture orbs with their equipment and others do not. Regular cameras, infrared cameras, and video equipment are best in capturing or seeing orbs.

FALSE ORBS. What does a false orb look like? Most but not all false orbs are round with a translucent center. I would like to caution you that not all translucent orbs are fake. Orbs are not always white in color and can give clues about "who" or "what" is present.

How can false orbs be created? False orbs can be created by a flash bounce against a shiny or hard surface creating a round circle with what may appear to be a translucent mass. When the flash bounces off of something reflective in the air, it may be the result of dust, bugs, or other particles that may also include raindrops, humidity, or ice crystals. Orbs can also be created by gases from decomposition of plants, human or animal remains, or types of organisms that survive in swamp water.

How does one know if what they have captured is something real? The answer to this question lies in analyzing your conditions: (1) What is the weather like? (2) What is the moon phase that day? (3) What are the environmental conditions like around you (dusty, humid, bugs, etc.)? (4) What is the temperature in and outside of a building? and, (5) Are you experiencing other unusual cues in your situation such as unexplainable sounds, smells, touch, and movement of objects?

REAL ORBS BRING MESSAGES

As I continue to study the paranormal field, I have been able to sensitize myself to detail in the environment that would generally go unnoticed. Capturing orbs has strengthened my ability to be an effective investigator. My being able to determine whether an orb is fake or real in my pictures has helped me understand the messages relayed to me by unknown entities in unexplained situations. In the images I am about to show you, you will see how orbs can relay important messages about others, particularly when it may involve health, situation, or presence of a guardian angel.

DEFINITIONS

Agent – a living agent who is the focus of paranormal activity. **Anomaly** – something that cannot be explained. For example, an orb that is not the result of a camera mishap or caused by external factors such as dust, bugs, moisture, reflections, and gas emissions. **Gases** – decomposition and swamp gases that have the ability to appear as floating orbs. **Infrared Camera** – a special filter incorporated within camera that allows photography or filming in low light conditions capturing what cannot be visually seen.

Orb – a commonly photographed circle or ball of energy that theoretically represents the "spirit" of a deceased person or animal. Often appears as a ball of light on film not often seen with the naked eye at the time of capture. Can appear in different sizes, color, density, shape, motion, and flexibility. False orbs can be dust, moisture, insects, or lens reflections. **Orb Color** – orb color is interpreted to be its "emotional" state of the entity. **Sensitive** – a person who possesses extrasensory talents.

ENCOUNTER
The Orb Doctor

My sister and niece came to visit my husband and myself several years ago. We decided to travel around the state to various tourist locations stopping at a winery for a moment of rest. My sister has complained for years that she felt like there was a hole in her airway located in her chest when she breathed, making her feel tired. When she was born, she had a hole in her heart but was told it would close-up and heal over time. No doctor has been able to determine what her health issue is. She says it feels as if there is a "leak" somewhere in the middle of her chest to the point where sometimes, the area "whistles." As we were sitting at the picnic bench, I decided to shoot some random pictures. Look at where the orb is located on her chest. It is in the area where she has complained. There is no explanation how an orb would show up during daylight captured on print film [no flash].

REVIEW OF IMAGE. A filter was applied to the image so you could see the orb over her chest. The orb is semi-solid, not translucent. From an investigative viewpoint, three factors are apparent in review of this round orb that showed on my sister's chest: (1) the image was photographed using 400 ASA print film, (2) the picture was taken in daylight with no flash (not common to capture an orb in daylight or shade with film that is not sensitive enough), and (3) the orb is over her chest/heart area. One should also note that the orb is not SOLID. Usually, SOLID

Photo with Applied Filter by Kelly Renee Schutz

orbs indicate the presence of something real. However, this capture offers an explanation about translucent orbs also being real. Not all translucent orbs are fake and can show up in low light conditions without a flash. The print film was inspected and there was no defect. The image was clearly embedded on her chest. I firmly believe this was meant to be a message or warning to her about her health condition.

As of this writing, my sister still has the feeling that there is a hole in her chest that "whistles" every time she breathes. She feels this sensation constantly. No doctor has been able to figure out what, if anything, is wrong with her. My recommendation for her would be to seek a specialist to determine what she is experiencing.

ENCOUNTER
Orb: Car Trade-In Approval

A friend of mine lost her husband several years ago to an illness. When a person loses their spouse, they are often faced with a confusing adjustment period. My friend told me that she had a difficult time navigating her deceased husband's truck and wanted to trade it in for a car. She struggled with this decision as she knew that her husband loved the truck.

On the day of her trade, you will notice in the picture that there is a HUGE sun flare shining over and around the truck (perhaps one of the biggest I have ever seen), and a large orb (see arrow) that is taking center stage.

Is this orb created by the sun as reflected on the hood of the car? Or, is her deceased husband trying to give her a sign of his approval for trading the truck in for a car that would be easier for her to drive?

Photo Courtesy of My Friend

ENCOUNTER
Orb: Sign from Guardian Angel?

During the end of the first week in December 2015, my husband and I left our home in Indiana (last minute) to take a road trip to West Virginia to look at a potential job site. I had applied for a position at a college and was asked to participate in the first round of phone interviews to take place that next week. Not sure of whether I wanted to move to this state, I asked my husband if he would take a last-minute road trip with me to see where the position was located. The total distance from our home to this job site was approximately 460 miles. I wanted to assure myself that this opportunity was a right move for me (he would remain at our present home), should I have been offered a 2nd interview, and potentially, the position.

Quick decision road trips can bring issues such as construction delays and unexpected situations, like accidents. Since we were traveling late into the evening, our first concern was neither of those but rather, being tired after a long week. My husband reviewed the weather application map and said, "crystal clear." This would be our first RED FLAG. We entered the address of the hotel we would be staying at into our GPS and off we went hoping to arrive by 11:30 PM.

Trusting in our GPS system, we began our journey with an uneventful trip through Ohio but noticed few cars and trucks on the road. This would be our second RED FLAG. We eventually ran into heavy fog (no advisory warning) finding ourselves slowing our travel plans to reach our hotel closer to midnight. This would be our third RED FLAG. To calm our nerves and feeling of isolation on a dark highway with few around us, we turned our radio station to a channel that was playing Christmas music. As this occurred, we noticed two police cars on the left side of the road sweeping up what appeared to be debris from an accident. This would be our fourth RED FLAG. We both commented we needed to watch our speed. All I could think about during this time was how "odd" it felt to be one of few on the road. This would be our fifth RED FLAG.

About 120 miles from our destination, we stopped at a truck stop to fill up with gasoline and use the restroom. As we were checking out with our purchases, a "buzz" about the fog was the talk among the employees and travelers around us. Someone would comment that it was clear about 30 miles up the road. This would be our sixth RED FLAG.

It would be about 10:45 PM (about 60 miles from our hotel) when the "dark conditions" would start to make me anxious. So, I turned on the radio back on and a Christmas song began to play by Dean Martin. As we inclined up a steep hill in clear conditions, we would comment to one another about Dean Martin and how we didn't have much further to go. All of a sudden and without warning ... out of nowhere and in seemingly SLOW MOTION ... I saw a 6-Point Buck (deer) appear on the left side of the road and walk without hesitation to the middle of the highway.

THE ACCIDENT. My husband shouts, "STOP THE CAR !!! WATCH OUT !!!" (Me) "HANG ON, WE ARE GOING TO HIT IT !!!!" [SMASH].

SLOW MOTION ... If I would have swerved the vehicle away from the deer as it was blocking the entire road, we could have ended up off the road tipped over, hitting a tree, hitting solid rock, etc. and might not have been seen or found until the next morning.

Because it was so dark out, I had no perspective of my surroundings when the deer entered the middle of the road. The most logical thing I could do at the time was to HIT THE DEER. They say if you are faced in a situation like this to slow the vehicle as fast as you can and hit the deer "straight on." I think I hit the deer around 20 or 30 miles per hour.

Just before impact, I shut my eyes. When I opened them (at impact), I thought I saw the legs of the deer flying off of its body in all directions (it was really the front bumper breaking into pieces) and the deer's carcass sliding down the highway in rapid speed.

HOW THE BRAIN REACTS. Fortunately, the air bags were not deployed as they could have caused internal injuries. Both of us, mildly traumatized from this event were thankful to be alive. Now we sat on the road in pitch dark. This felt unnerving. Although it felt like help was never going to arrive, we remained on the phone system with OnStar until the police came.

Driving our SUV on this trip was perhaps what saved us. *Or did something else save us?* We were fortunate the deer did not land on top of our hood coming through our windshield. Instead, the deer went right into the radiator and then bounced off being propelled forward. When impact was made with the deer, it felt like I was hitting a hollow drum (a 6-point buck is not a hollow drum). If we had hit a bear or wild turkey, the damage could have been much greater as well as life threatening.

TWO POLICE CARS. After contacting OnStar, we sat on the road for 15 minutes in the pitch dark awaiting the State Police to arrive (felt like forever). As we watched a handful of cars and large trucks pass us by, a young man had stopped to come to our aid. Keep in mind that we were in a strange place, it was pitch dark, we were vulnerable, and highway killings are not unheard of. Therefore, kept our windows rolled up and remained online with OnStar.

When the highway patrol finally arrived, he could not stay because there was another accident with injuries ahead of us. So, we sat on the highway for another 15 minutes awaiting the next State Police to show up. With a tow truck on its way, we eventually received the assistance we needed, loaded the vehicle onto the truck, and with 60 miles to go (yes, we proceeded to our hotel), we arrived around 1:30 AM after dropping the car off at the collision center.

ORB SHOWS UP. I had taken several photos of the damaged vehicle to this point. Pictures were clear in all angles. As the car was about to be unloaded at the collision center, what would take me by surprise would be an ORB that showed up in one of the pictures. With the night being crystal clear and the moon as bright as could be, where did this ORB come from? Who is this ORB? Was this the ORB of the deceased deer? Or, was this ORB a guardian angel?

Photo with Applied Filter by Kelly Renee Schutz

FILTERED IMAGE. A filter was applied to the image to bring out the ORB shape and inner mass appearance. Not all real ORBS have the same mass design inside of them. Not all real orbs are solid. This orb was semi-solid. Not all orbs are round.

WHO OR WHAT IS THIS ORB? I do not know "what" this orb is. I will speculate that this orb is the soul of "something." Whether it was the deer, a guardian angel, or someone who passed away in the neighborhood, all I know is that it showed up, allowing me to photograph it while watching it depart (in my photo).

WHAT THIS ORB IS NOT. This orb is not: (1) fake – dust, bugs, ice crystals, or a reflection; (2) it is not the moon, and, (3) it is not entirely round, which generally indicates injury or illness. No ORBS showed up in my other pictures under the same conditions.

This orb is not a reflection from inside the dealership (see light) or outside from the bumper (see glare). In a closer look at the orb (enlarged on my computer), the mass inside is semi-solid and is very bright, representing potential energy.

QUESTIONS / THOUGHTS

Do animals have a soul? How long does a soul hang on after its death? Where does this soul go? Some of my ghost psychic experts have told me that when a person dies, the soul rises no more than 3-5 feet above their body. What about animal souls?

The deer died on impact and suddenly. Was this ORB a sign that the deer was letting go? My ghost psychic expert told me that a soul (animal and human) can hang on for 1-4 hours before letting go. Or, was this ORB a guardian angel showing its presence? After all, this accident could have been deadly. These questions may never be answered.

Chapter 21
Tomatoes Jumping Off of Shelf

Illustration by Brandy Woods

Chapter 21
Tomatoes Jumping Off of Shelf

PHENOMENA

You are walking down an aisle in the produce section of a grocery store when a small carton of yellow tomatoes JUMP off a shelf directly in front of you landing in the middle of the aisle. Startled, you pause for a moment to try and figure out how this could have occurred. Later that same day, as you sleep in bed, your television turns on by itself with no explanation causing both of you to panic.

In two of my chapters written in Book 1 entitled, *Behind the Curtain <u>and Book Flying Off Shelf</u>*, I wrote about how a jar filled with baby teeth jumped at me unexpectedly on a table I was standing next while I was involved in an estate picking. In the other chapter, I wrote about how a book flew off a shelf intended to hit my administrator. In this chapter in this book, I will write about how a small tub of yellow cherry tomatoes jumped off of a shelf in front of my husband with no logical explanation.

MOON PHASES. What do a new moon, full moon, blood moon, and a super moon all have in common? They provide an energy field strong enough to manifest unexplained phenomena. Over the years, it has been apparent to my husband and me that when he questions whether ghosts exist, that something odd will happen to him. How do you explain objects that "fly off of" walls or "jump" off tables or shelves? This is a difficult question to answer.

DEFINITIONS

Agent – a living person who is the focus of paranormal activity. **Collective Apparition** – a rare type of sighting in which more than one person sees the same apparition or phenomena. **Energy Lines** - lines that crisscross the earth like a spider webs and where they come together to create energy centers. Energy lines increase paranormal activity (resemble vortexes in pictures) because they increase energy vibrations. Energy lines show different colors. **Illusion** – a perception between what is perceived and what is reality. **Intelligent Haunting** – interaction on the physical plane as in communication or object movement from a spirit who is conscious. **Moon Phases** – people associate moon phases with episodes of paranormal activity. Moon phases are favorable for ghost hunting because their energy fields are at their strongest. The best time to experience paranormal phenomena is two to three days before, during, or after a moon phase. **Super Moon** – a super moon occurred on September 27-28, 2015; also known as the biggest, brightest, and closest moon of the year.

ENCOUNTER

On a clear afternoon one September 27, 2015 day, my husband and I decided to go grocery shopping. On our way to the market, I commented to him that we were going to have a "super moon" that evening. Super moons, as compared to all other moon phases, have stronger energy fields, especially on clear nights. My husband had his doubts we would encounter anything that evening and rolled his eyes at the idea that moon phases created energy.

As we entered the grocery store, we began our shopping by first going into the produce department. Oddly, we noticed we were the only ones in this department. We decided to split up to make our shopping process go faster.

JUMPING TOMATOES. It was probably no more than 10 seconds after we split up that I heard him say loudly, "WHAT THE HECK" (forcing me to turn back to look in his direction). As I turned around, I noticed he was kneeling on the floor. My initial thought was that he was physically ill perhaps having a heart attack.

Shaking this confusion off, I was puzzled to see him picking up off the floor, a small container of yellow cherry tomatoes (lid intact). "WHAT DID YOU DO?" I couldn't help my reaction as it is one of my usual blame comments. [Me] "Did you knock those tomatoes off the shelf?" [Him] "No." [Me] "Did they fall off the shelf by themselves?" [Him] "No." [Me] "Well then, why are you picking a carton of tomatoes off the floor?" Oddly enough, the container didn't break and it landed face up (about 3 feet into the aisle).

My husband, startled, told me that the tomatoes jumped off the shelf right in front of him. My reaction then turned to puzzlement and more questioning. [Me] "You mean to tell me that the tomatoes JUMPED off the shelf right in front of you?" He said, "Yes." [Me] "Are you sure?" [Him] "Yes." [Me] "Are you sure they didn't just topple over and fall due to vibration?" [Him] "No, they actually flew out in front of me … in fact I thought they were going to hit me." My final reaction was, "no comment" (thinking to myself, "cool").

Most people would have freaked out and left the store. I considered this moment to be an odd validation proving to my husband that strong energy fields are real on moon phase days. Could the tomatoes have been near an energy line? Or, was a poltergeist trying to prove a point to him? What caused these tomatoes to "jump" off the shelf with no vibration or movement of its shelf?

REASONS. Here are a few reasons as to why I feel this moment was unusually paranormal: (1) we were in the produce department alone, (2) we split up making the incident viewed by 1 person, and (3) the tomatoes "jumped" off the shelf and didn't simply "fall" off the shelf. Ghostly activity does not always occur in the presence of more than one person. Ghostly activity can happen quickly and without warning causing confusion. And, the environmental conditions (energy field) was right for manifestation.

Unfortunately, as much as I wanted to approach the manager to see if we could view the video coverage of this incident, this was probably not allowed and would be considered an "odd" request. As we continued with our shopping, I said to my husband, "next time, do not challenge or doubt that activity does not occur during a super moon day/evening." If this were paranormal involving an entity, something was obviously provoked by his comment. If this were an energy line, the timing of it was coincidentally spot on.

ENCOUNTER #2

TV TURNS ON BY ITSELF. Flustered and confused by the tomato incident in the grocery market that afternoon, we shook it off, chocked it up for an interesting experience, and went to bed around midnight.

For some reason, I had a nagging feeling that something else was yet to happen. I laid in bed wide awake until around 1:00 AM. After all, if tomatoes were jumping off a shelf in the early evening, I could only imagine how strong the energy fields would be after midnight causing other events to manifest.

What I was most paranoid about the most was the haunted farmstead across the road. Skies were crystal clear and the moon was very bright. Perfect conditions for manifestations.

AFTER 2:00 AM. It was just after midnight, around 2:00-2:30 AM (September 28), with the super moon at its strongest when we were awakened from our sleep to find our TELEVISION turned on in our master bedroom. We rarely watched TV in our master bedroom and never experienced any frequency interferences of neighbor's televisions since moving in. My immediate reaction was to locate the remote (thinking I turned the TV on in my sleep). However, I found the remote in its usual position untouched on the nightstand on my side of the bed. This is the point where we both felt paranoid while mumbling to another, "you don't suppose we have visitors from across the road tonight, do you?" We went back to sleep.

QUESTIONS / THOUGHTS

Who or what threw the tomatoes in front of my husband at the grocery store? This wasn't my first seeing objects "jump" out in my presence. It felt to me to be an entity over an energy line because the timing was oddly coincidental. My husband had just made a remark about not believing in moon phases causing paranormal activity which provoked a situation to occur. Do I think something followed us into the grocery store? Possibly. I have ghosts near me daily.

FREQUENCY? Why did our television turn on by itself? We believe it was not because of a neighbor's television frequency. Why not? Because we have never had our television turn on like this before or after that evening. Occurred on a full moon evening.

TV BECOMES NEW ROUTINE. My husband put batteries into the dead anniversary clock so I would not be able to tell when we were having a paranormal moment. The dead clock would move on full moon evenings as a sign of a presence. On April 20, 2016, as we were napping in our livingroom, our TV turned off by itself with no known power outage or frequency issue. It seems as though our ghostly guests like to play with our TV on full moon days/evenings – turning it "on and off" ... especially when we are sleeping.

Chapter 22
Haunted Pioneer Saloon

Photo Illustration by Kelly Renee Schutz

Pioneer Saloon, Goodsprings, Nevada
August 2014 and August 2016

Chapter 22
Haunted Pioneer Saloon

PHENOMENA

In 1860, Joseph Good, who established the town of Goodsprings, Nevada, found fresh water in the area and planted cottonwood trees. As the town began to grow and flourish, people came from miles around to shop and entertain themselves there. The *Pioneer Saloon*, one of its buildings, is ONE of many known haunted buildings in the area. The *Pioneer Saloon* is located approximately 30-35 miles outside of Las Vegas, Nevada. The saloon became famously known when Clark Gable drank at this bar awaiting the news of his deceased wife, Jane Alice Peters, known as Carole Lombard, who died in a plane crash on a mountain that could be seen from the saloon on January 16, 1942.[2]

GHOSTS IN SALOON. Carol Lombard, actress, and a few other resident ghosts are alleged to be haunting the saloon. The old miner ghost is believed to be that of an old prospector in his early 70's who has been observed sitting at the bar. Another ghost, a gambler by the name of Paul, is believed to have cheated at a card game and was shot 6 times by another gambler. He lied dead in a side door of the saloon for 10 hours before he was removed. He appears to hang out in the lounge area of the saloon. It is believed the gambler was shot on July 3, 1913.[2] Ruby, a female ghost, who was a waitress during that same period, was mistaken for being a prostitute and was killed by an aggressive patron who visited the bar, killing her in the women's restroom.

TOM. Just down the road a short distance from the saloon is a rundown shack, originally built by Mr. Campbell in 1896, that continues to be haunted by a miner named A.E. Thomas. Tom lived in this cabin for 2 years before he contracted and died of the Spanish flu. He was found decomposed in his bed after going unnoticed for several months. Tom is picky about who he interacts with when visitors or tour guides stop by. He often communicates through a radio control device (REM). If he is angry, he will tell those he dislikes to LEAVE or has been known to take possession of someone's vulnerable body speaking through them with his warning to LEAVE often causing the individual to faint on the ground. Agnes, a lady friend of his, has been reported to visit him.

HAUNTED SALOON AND SCHOOLHOUSE

The historical landmark, *Pioneer Saloon*, was reported to have been built in 1913 by a prominent business man named George Faylepast.[2] The interior and exterior walls of the saloon remains original to date, made from stamped tin manufactured by Sears and Roebuck.[2] The *Pioneer Saloon* is thought to be one of the last mining ghost town saloons of its kind in the United States.² The legendary bar and foot rest rail, manufactured and installed in 1913 by the Brunswick Company (Maine) in the 1860's, remains in the saloon.²

According to the *Pioneer Saloon* website (2007), many movies have been filmed at the saloon but the genuine stories that were created here lived on beyond movie scripts echoing the past.² The famous screen legend, Clark Gable, waited for three days at the bar for word on his wife of less than two years Carole Lombard.² Carole Lombard was killed in a plane crash near Mount Potosi.

At one time, the saloon resided next to a hotel that not only served as a resting place for nearly 2500 prospectors and miners in the West, but also served as a place where nearly 250 street girls (prostitutes) would frequent with their clients.² The hotel was destroyed by a fire in 1966 when a drunk bartender threw something hot outside of a window causing it and leaving only ashes. In 2010, the population of Goodsprings was 229.²

In 2016, visitors who toured the *Pioneer Saloon* were able to see bullet holes from back in the early 1900's lodged in a wall that is directly across from the bar. Some of the bullet holes were from gun fights. An original potbellied stove and several paper clippings are found in the lounge area as a reminder of the Wild West.

SCHOOLHOUSE. The Goodsprings schoolhouse was built in 1913. It is located just down the road from the saloon. The schoolhouse is reported to be haunted by Katherine Williams, school teacher, and a number of children. Children are known to show up on occasion on site with the most common being Emily, Paulie, and Tommie (ages 4-12).

WALKING DOWN THE ROAD. In walking down a road that borders many of the haunted cabins in the area, one might have an experience with a young, redhead girl by the name of Mary (age 10-12), who shows herself by walking right next to them.

DEFINITIONS

Agent – a living person who is the focus of poltergeist activity. **Anomaly** – something that cannot be explained. For example, an orb that is not the result of a camera mishap or caused by external factors such as dust, bugs, moisture, reflections, and gas emissions. **Contact Session** – a period of time in which paranormal investigators attempt to establish communication with an entity. **Earthbound** – a ghost or spirit that is unable to cross over to the other side at the time of death and is stuck in this physical plane. **Entity** – anything that has a separate, distinct existence, though not necessarily material in nature. **Haunting** – a reoccurring ghostly phenomena that returns to a location where no one is physically present. **Intelligent Haunting** – an interaction on the physical plane as in communication or object movement. **Orb** – a translucent or solid spheres of light which dart erratically through the air. Most believe ghosts take an orb shape as it requires less energy than other apparitions. **Place-Centered Haunting** – a location where paranormal events frequently take place. **Mist** – a photographed anomaly that appears as a blanket of light (looks like fog). **Moon Phases** – a full moon is most favorable to ghost hunt because the energy fields are at their strongest (two to three days before, during, or after). **Moving Orb** – an orb that moves quickly showing a trail of light that emanates from the sphere.

ENCOUNTERS EXPERIENCED AUGUST 2014

My sister, young nephew (age 14), and I traveled to Las Vegas, Nevada on August 7-10, 2014 to enjoy a variety of activities and tours. Over the past 30 years, I had made my way to Las Vegas on numerous trips but never roamed outside of the city limits. Daytime temperatures in August were a blistering 105-110 degrees.

One of the activities we decided to share together during our trip was that of an interactive ghost hunting adventure originating in Goodsprings, Nevada. It was by luck and chance that we would be the only participants on this tour this evening. It was also by chance that it was to be the evening of a FULL MOON, known to have a strong energy field.

Getting on a small shuttle bus at the Royal Resort Hotel, Las Vegas, we travelled approximately 30 miles out into the desert from Vegas to Goodsprings, Nevada. As we drove through the flat, dry desert, we couldn't help but notice how golden the sun was this evening. We arrived at Goodsprings around 6:30 PM, we, along with several other stop by tourists (not part of the tour), enjoyed the saloon.

Protocol by most ghost tour guides who offered such a unique experience in Las Vegas was to begin by explaining a short history of the places we were to visit followed by an interactive experience. This was to be a 3-hour ghost hunting adventure. The excitement in being part of something claimed to be authentic was intriguing. It was hard not to compare this tour to others I had been on in the past. In the end, I would give this tour adventure 5 out of 5 stars.

ARRIVAL PIONEER SALOON. When we arrived at the *Pioneer Saloon,* we were guided into one of three small buildings and were given a brief tour of each of them. Busy with people, my first thought was that the energies of these people would scare off the ghostly entities. From my experiences, ghostly entities do not generally like to be active around crowds or groups of people.

HISTORY. A small saloon, the main building had two original areas – a bar and a sitting lounge. We began our adventure by sitting in the lounge, ordered a pizza, and listened to stories about the Carole Lombard plane crash, Clark Gable's visit to the saloon, the miners and gamblers who frequented the saloon, and finally, the demise or desertion of residents from the town.

INCIDENT 1 – MENS RESTROOM. While we were enjoying our pizza and listening to stories, our tour guide made mention that if we needed to use the restrooms to keep an eye out because the ghostly entities liked to haunt them. With my 14-year old nephew in need of going, I escorted him to the door of the men's restroom to ensure his safety. As we walked a short distance from the sitting lounge into the bar area, I couldn't help but notice a small crowd of people gathered at the bar, mingling with one another as well as points of interest such as a bullet hole in the tin wall and the aged furniture of the past. Walking across the creaky wooden plank floor provided a sound most common to what may have been heard in the past by visitors and locals alike.

As we reached the restroom, my nephew was nervous about going inside of it because it had no lock on the door. I told him I would guard the door and not let anyone past me. While standing around the door waiting for him, I noticed how small this saloon was but was intrigued by its western character.

I had stood outside the men's restroom no more than five minutes when my nephew came charging out of it right at me trembling with fright on his face. I said to him, "well, that was quick." I then noticed him trembling. "What's wrong?" He told me the light went off and on in the restroom. I said, "I have been standing out here the entire time and no one went in there to turn the switch off." Nephew said, "there is no switch on the wall, only a bulb fixed into the ceiling. And, it was slowly going off, flickered on, and then went off as I was doing my business."

SEE IMAGE ON THE NEXT PAGE.

SIDE NOTE: In August 2016, the poster was removed and the entire restroom was painted in BROWN. The original tin, as seen in the August 2014 image, remained but covered in paint. The only thing I captured during the August 2016 trip in here was my shadow (where poster is) giving off the impression I had captured a cowboy wearing a hat.

It was at this point my curiosity had gotten the best of me. I asked my nephew to open the door (see previous page). If you look inside the restroom, you will see that it is constructed with TIN or a type of METAL in its surround. This type of metal (see history of its construction) can absorb energy from inside and outside sources. As he slowly opened the door, sure enough, there was no switch on the wall. The bulb was on the ceiling too high to be reached. I turned to him and said, "the light is on." He responded, "it shut off while I was trying to go." I said, "for

Photo taken by Kelly Renee Schutz
Looking Inside the Men's Restroom, Pioneer Saloon

Image in August 2014

how long?" He said, "it felt like 5 minutes, I couldn't see anything." I do recall when he opened the door that the light was off and suddenly came back on. Perhaps the light was on a timer? No. Motion sensor? No. As I peered at the light from outside the door, I noticed it was not flickering with movement and was very bright. We went back to the sitting lounge where I asked the tour guides some specific questions about the construction of the restroom and building.

ATTEMPT TO DEBUNK

If I were to attempt to DEBUNK this moment and claim it as NOT being paranormal, I would consider the following: (1) was the light bulb loose where it had an occasional connection failure? (2) did the restroom have a motion sensor that turned the bulb off and on to reduce burning out while conserving energy? (3) did the 100-ear old building have occasional electrical issues causing the bulb to go out? (4) was there anyone standing above the men's restroom (roof or 2nd floor) walking around causing the bulb to loosen? (5) was there someone playing a practical joke on my nephew by telling him that the restroom was haunted but toying with him by playing tricks with the lights?

FACTS

Here are the facts that were relayed to me. First, the entire building was on the same electrical wiring. Second, the bulb in the restroom remained on continuously and was not on a timer or triggered by motion. Third, a new bulb had just been put in. Fourth, no one would have wasted their time playing pranks on a young boy who needed to use the restroom. Fifth, the roof was above the restroom with no one standing on it. Sixth, we were experiencing a full moon evening involving a strong energy field which aids in manifestations. Seventh, the metals in the ground and building were conductors in absorbing energy (essential for manifestations).

THEREFORE, knowing the history that resident ghosts make visits on occasion to the Pioneer Saloon, knowing the place had busy energy from visitors, knowing we were in a full moon phase, knowing the building was made of materials that absorbed energy and manifested apparitions, and knowing the electric of that building was all wired together convinces me enough to declare that what my nephew experienced was an unexplained paranormal encounter by someone, suspected to be the gambler or miner.

LADIES RESTROOM. At the point where I had brought my nephew back to the sitting lounge (where we were eating pizza and listening to stories), I decided to take my camera into the ladies' restroom to see if I could capture any activity. I captured a few orbs (see image next page). In review of them on my computer, it was determined that the upper right corner orb (solid) is real and the others within the frame are potentially light reflections from the paint used on the wall. How can I determine the orb in the right corner is real? It has a solid mass and is different from the others.

IMAGE 3 – ORBS IN LADIES RESTROOM.

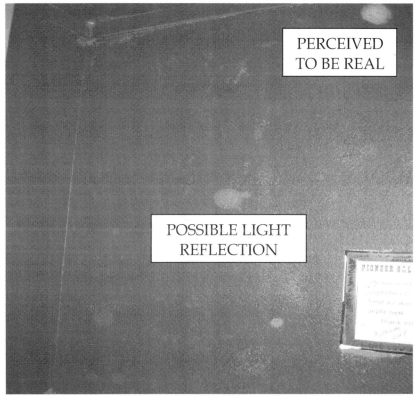

Photo Taken by Kelly Renee Schutz

Although not all semi-translucent orbs are fake, what is apparent in this picture is that many of these orbs were created from the type of paint used on the wall. Nothing captured in August 2016.

INCIDENT 2 – THE GAMBLING EXPERIENCE. After we were done eating our pizza, we continued to sit in the lounge at the original poker table (wooden) attempting to replicate the evening one of the gamblers was shot when he was caught cheating at poker. Acting as gamblers, we used trigger objects to elicit a reaction. We held a few gaming cards in our hands, threw a few poker chips on the table, and had a fake bottle of whiskey on the table. We asked questions while monitoring our meters, recorders, and cameras.

With our meters lighting up as a reaction to our questions, our ghost radar devices relaying words, and my K-2 meter (far right in picture) lighting up to 5 buttons, it would give a false presumption that we were experiencing activity. Even though this moment was interesting, it was not convincing enough for me to believe we were in the presence of one or more ghosts because there were too many people roaming around inside the room and building. We left the building to drive to a few haunted miner shacks and old schoolhouse.

INCIDENT 3 – GUARDED BY MIST. As we traveled from one miner shack to another, we would take pictures to attempt to capture moving orbs or mists. We also used our Ghost Radar Pro Meters (one blink for yes and two blinks for no) when asking questions as well as a REM Pod (acts as a radio transmitter where it scrolls through multiple channels picking up words). If an apparition wanted to speak to us, its words would be instinct with our questions.

LARGE ORANGE ORBS (MIST) = "Protection" and "Forgiveness"

PICTURE PREVIOUS PAGE. Using a 2-snap picture shooting approach, I was able to capture a HEAVY mist at one of the miner's shacks (see pictures that follow). Picture below shows a heavy MIST mass compiled of several large ORANGE orbs coming to me. Large orbs represent the age of an entity. The other picture (next page), same image, shot 10 seconds later, shows nothing.

SAME IMAGE 10 SECONDS LATER = Shows No Orbs or Mist. How is it that mist can show up on one image and seconds later ... disappear? Some people would argue this is a weather-related occurrence. I argue that it is not coincidental and is not of a typical nature.

Photo Taken by Kelly Renee Schutz

INCIDENT 4 – MIST AND ORB IN MOTION. See Images Next Pages. In traveling to another miner shack, I captured the images that follow by putting my camera through a thin crack inside an outside wall and snapping 2 pictures in a row (quickly). What you see in **Image 1** is MIST and in **Image 2,** an ORB IN MOTION. It is difficult to determine if the ORB IN MOTION manifested from the MIST. Orbs travel very quickly in a circular form.

Your first impression might be that the mist is a glow from reflections off the wood. However, in comparing Image 1 to Image 2, you will see this is not the case. **IMAGE 1 = MIST.** Resembles a smoky or cloudy interior.

Photo Taken by Kelly Renee Schutz

IMAGE 2 = ORB IN MOTION. See next image. Same picture. Was taken 5-10 seconds after Image 1. The **light flash** in the middle of the shack in front of you is from my camera. The moving orb to the left is attempting to leave the building from the side. See how clear Image 2 is as compared to Image 1?

IMAGE 2 = MIST WITH MOVING ORB. Same Image **Seconds Later.** See how clear this image is as compared to the other?

Photo Taken by Kelly Renee Schutz

CAPTURING ORBS. Orbs are most commonly seen as circular (round) with a solid or translucent mass in its center. Some orbs can take different shapes (oblong or partial). If an orb is SOLID, the likelihood it is REAL is greater than if it were translucent. However, not all translucent orbs are fake. The consensus by paranormal investigators is that orbs are dust particles in the air, bugs, moisture, raindrops, snowflakes, light bounce reflections off shiny surfaces, or gases emitted from swamps.

SIDE NOTE: It is interesting to note that many of the orbs I have captured using my digital camera, especially those that are real, have an unusual behavior pattern. Many of them give the appearance that they are HIDING - either in the upper, side, or lower frames of the picture. When I enlarge these orbs on my computer (to review their inner masses), I find the most authentic ones to be: (1) solid, (2) very bright mass, and (3) never having the same pattern as others I have captured. Translucent orbs are much harder to determine if they are real.

QUESTIONS / THOUGHTS

What is it about the *Pioneer Saloon* that allows for the manifestation of apparitions? I believe the answer lies in the sudden trauma experienced there as well as the elements that have stored energy, such as the metal construction of buildings.

Do apparitions show themselves to everyone on this tour? I'm not entirely sure. We were there on a full moon weekend which allowed for capturing some very interesting manifestations. I enjoyed capturing the moving orb and mist in some of the shacks.

Would I recommend this tour to children under the age of 14? No. Generally, kids under 18 are not allowed to participate in this tour for two reasons: (1) alcohol in environment, and (2) may become too scared. My nephew was given permission to participate on this tour because he was with two experienced adults who understood paranormal situations. Have any tourists experienced anything more than capturing orbs and mists on this tour? Yes.

Continue reading what happened to one of our tour guides, a couple from the Netherlands, and my husband/myself when we went on this tour in June 2016 on a NEW MOON evening.

<u>SIDE NOTE:</u> CEMETERY. True story. While out in the middle of nowhere investigating a cemetery, all the doors of the tour van suddenly locked with no spare keys to get back into the vehicle. Moments later, the apparition(s) unlocked the doors.

Illustration by Brandy Woods

ENCOUNTERS EXPERIENCED ON AUGUST 1, 2016
This would be my second time experiencing this tour and the first time for my husband. What you experience on this tour is never the same. You never know what to expect. It was not planned that we would be doing this tour on a NEW MOON evening. Not only was the energy strong that evening, it was STRONGER than the FULL MOON evening we experienced early August 2014.

COUPLE FROM THE NETHERLANDS

A couple from the Netherlands participated on this tour with my husband and myself this evening (August 1, 2016). We were a small group of four accompanied by two tour guides. The couple from the Netherlands provided me with images they took with their cell phones while on this tour (THANK YOU). You will see some of their images on the pages that follow. All verified as hard evidence. This was their first time being on a tour like this and did not know what to expect.

CAPTURES OF EVIDENCE

Compared to my experiences in August 2014, this evening would be the more intense. When we visited Tom's cabin, it was apparent he was not happy to see any of us (August 2014, he was cooperative and nice). Tom did not like our tour guide (new) and was clear about not wanting to speak to him through the REM machine. On occasion, Tom would ask for the former tour guide "by her name" – as communicated through the REM machine. Tom had said many times that he wanted us to LEAVE. Tom would get very angry and annoyed when we shined our flashlights on his cabin. I believe it was "TOM" who I captured standing at his front door at the point when we were leaving (see next page). Orb is round and solid. I had cut off the top of the picture where other orbs were noticed to focus on the orb in the door. It is believed that Tom enjoyed the company of others, including a lady friend by the name of Agnes, who visited him on occasion.

Photo Illustration by Kelly Schutz

CABIN WITH CIGAR MAN

Once we left Tom's cabin, we went to another cabin. It was here that our tour guide told us that he was an empath (could see dead people) and at one point, told me to shoot photographs in the direction he pointed. He described what he saw as an elderly man wearing a floppy hat smoking a cigar standing between the building and a tree. At first, I didn't believe him. That was until I shot this image below. I know this image is difficult to see but the arrows are pointing to "legitimate" orbs – they are not reflections, dust, or bugs. The timing of his command followed by my timing in taking the picture was too coincidental. Do not know if the energy ball "split" or if there were others watching us while we were standing there. See arrow on bottom pointing to orb.

Photo Illustration by Kelly Schutz

ENERGY BALL FOLLOWS US

As we were walking away from this building, we stopped at another cabin. The tour guide mentioned he had not made contact with anything at this cabin for nearly eight months. It just so happens that as we continued to walk, I turned around and shot this image (orb in motion) on my camera. See image next page.

Photo Illustration by Kelly Schutz

When you look at this picture above, you will see a very large orb near center. You are not able to see clearly enough that it is in MOTION ... and it is either shooting upward or downward (creating a path). It is by chance that I managed to photograph this same orb on my video camera using an ultraviolet lens. An ultraviolet lens can see what WE CANNOT SEE. On my video coverage, this orb flew over my head, walked right next to the assistant tour guide, and then, BLOCKED the view of the Netherlands couple, who attempted to take pictures of the POST OFFICE. See images on the next page.

Photo Illustration by Netherlands Couple

The image above is REAL and is an AMAZING capture. It is the SAME ORB that I captured on my camera you see on the page before this one. I also captured this orb on VIDEO using my ultraviolet lens at the cabin we just left following it to this area. The Netherlands couple, including myself, did not see this orb at the time of shooting. They shot 7-8 pictures in a row non-stop and this image showed in every single frame not allowing them to take a picture of the Post Office. This is ONE STUBBORN ORB in motion.

When an image like this is taken (see above), this is a VERY STRONG energy ball. You will see that the Post Office is clear. We do not know WHY this motion orb reluctantly wanted to BLOCK their images.

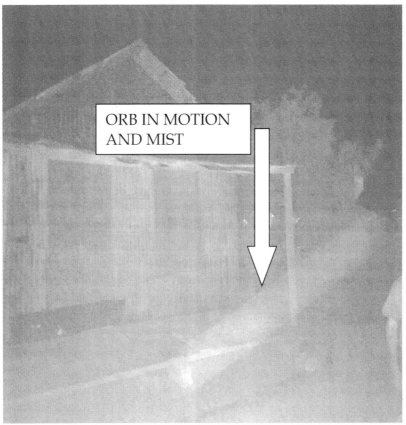

Photo Illustration by Netherlands Couple
Post Office

In the image above, you will notice TWO things. First, you will see the MOTION ORB in action. Image was taken with a cell phone. Next, you will notice a WHITE CLOUDY

MIST. Their phone cameras were so sensitive that they were able to capture the ectoplasmic mist that attempted to BLOCK their being able to take a picture of the POST OFFICE. This is not dust and you will see that the post office image is clearly captured.

STONE BUILDING DESTINATION

The most intense moment of the evening was when we were on our way to the stone building destination. Before we even stopped the van to get out, my flashlight battery had gone completely dead. I know that I pestered Tom with my shutting it off and on at his cabin. I had wondered if he or something else (the motion orb that followed us to the post office) had anything to do with it. In the image below, you will see TWO orbs around the tour guide's head following him to the stone building.

Photo Illustration by Kelly Schutz

Since our tour guide was an empath (could see dead people) and I am extremely open and sensitive to paranormal entities, it was of no surprise that we attracted a crowd that evening.

Photo Illustration by Netherlands Couple

What you see in the image above is just outside the stone building. SEVERAL orbs are in motion. They had surrounded us and this stone building before we stepped foot into it. The area was completely infested with energy orbs that evening. I personally could not feel anything while we were there. However, what you see above IS AN AMAZING CAPTURE. When we were inside the cabin, our tour guide attempted contact with two of the deceased boys who were being held prisoner (Christopher, age 12 and Kenny, age 8. Edward, in his mid-20's and former child offender, was holding these boys hostage inside this stone building.

The boys often huddled in a corner inside the cabin in fear of Edward. While we were in there, our tour guide attempted to make contact with the boys using his REM machine. He had just made contact with Kenny when Edward interfered telling him (us) to LEAVE. As we stood in the pitch dark listening to these messages, the anger grew more intense as the tour guide refused to leave. It was at this moment that Edward decided to cause the assistant tour guide to FAINT onto the floor. Keep in mind that she was perhaps the most fragile of all of us, wasn't protected enough, and didn't wear a cross. She hit the floor faster than a lightning bolt. It was at this point that we all left.

Situations like this are dangerous. Provoking ghosts is not what a person should ever do, especially if you are not experienced in understanding their capabilities. At the point of her fainting, the Netherlands couple dragged her out of the cabin holding both of her arms helping her back into the van.

When we arrived back to the saloon, the fainting tour guide still felt weak and dizzy. The Netherlands woman felt tingling all over her body. I had wondered if I was in a position to help either should both of them be in need of my help. The tour guide was insistent we keep things moving as we were behind schedule and the saloon was about to close up for the night.

Inside the saloon, we re-enacted the gambling scene, where Paul got shot, and then, left, driving back to Vegas stopping at the final destination, the Cemetery, before calling it a night. See image on next page.

CEMETERY

During my August 2014 visit to this cemetery while on this tour, I had captured nothing. During this visit, I was able to SEE many orb entities in my camera (infrared light) while taking photographs. No one had walked in this cemetery prior to our arrival to create dust. What you see on the next page are not bugs. What you see is an orb shower.

This would be my second time capturing an orb shower. Who are these entities? They could be transient orbs (from everywhere) who realized some of us were sensitive and decided to come for a visit. We had been surrounded all night by activity that this was of no surprise to see such a gathering.

A few of these entities hitched a ride back with us as we left. I know this because I felt sick in the van and somewhat dizzy. I was not about to say anything because I didn't want to cause any alarm. It just so happens that the next day in my hotel room, I found myself coming out of a trance while standing in the shower. My husband had come into the bathroom to check on me because the water was running so long. When he arrived, I snapped out of it and felt an intense cold feeling rising from my toes going throughout my body leaving my head. I have never had such a strong feeling like this before.

Photo Illustration by Kelly Schutz

When I captured this image, I was standing alone away from the others. No one had been in this area prior to kick up dust prior to my standing there. The ORB in the middle (solid white) is not only real but very strong. When I clicked half way down on my camera, I noticed in the viewer (infra-red light) that it looked like a bunch of SALT was being throw at me ... so, in essence, my infra-red light captured several and this is the result.

Chapter 23
The Basement Ghost

Illustration by Brandy Woods

Chapter 23
The Basement Ghost

PHENOMENA

A bottle smashes against a wall in the basement cellar. You hear footsteps walking away after the bottle breaks.

A voice of a deceased miner who fell to his death in a mining hole in the basement cellar is answering specific questions through the use of a spirit box (frequency sweep radio). He likes ice cream.

A flashlight blinks on and off to your command in the pool hall. A pool ball moves across the table without assistance or vibration.

There are movements of objects on the main floor by the bar. Lights turn on and off by themselves. Gambling wheel spins on its own. Cards and poker chips fly off a wooden table.

Phantom cowboys are seen at the bar while others walk around the saloon. The ghost of Big Nose Kate continues to lurk around in the building as this was one of her favorite places to visit.

It would appear one or more ghosts like the comfort of hanging around the Crystal Palace and Saloon Restaurant, located in Tombstone, Arizona.

HISTORY OF THE CRYSTAL PALACE AND SALOON

Originally known as the Golden Eagle Brewing Company, this establishment was one of early Tombstone's first saloons.[3] The saloon occupied a small lot of about 50 by 30 feet while the brewery was in another structure to the rear. Named after its builder, Benjamin Wehrfritz, the Wehrfritz Building was expanded by adding a second story to house the offices for such notables as U.S. Deputy Marshal Virgil Earp, attorney George W. Berry, and Dr. George E. Goodfellow. It is even known that "Buckskin" Frank Leslie was a night watchman here for a short time![3]

The Golden Eagle Brewery was not hit as hard as others in Tombstone when the June 22, 1881 fire swept through town, leaving in its wake a mass of destroyed buildings. During this fire, a large bucket brigade helped save this building from total destruction. Fire was soon to be the demise of this once two-story building when on May 26, 1882 is was totally destroyed as flames swept through and took with it all that was once the Golden Eagle Brewery.[3]

Swift action saw to it that the saloon was quickly rebuilt and the name was changed to the Crystal Palace Saloon. Imagine as you sit here and gaze around this fine establishment that in the center of the room was a goldfish pond "which spouts forth streams of pure water" as stated in the Tombstone Epitaph of July 23, 1882.[3]

The Crystal Palace Saloon soon became known as a fine dining establishment that not only served oysters and other delicacies in the lunchroom of the Palace, but also boasted of carrying the choicest brands of wines, liquors, and cigars.[3] Gambling and live music were also part of the action every night of the week.

Prohibition saw another incarnation of the Crystal Palace Saloon and gambling laws soon made what was once a normal part of life in Tombstone soon a piece of the past. It is said that a businessman purchased the roulette wheels, gambling tables, and later the bar, and fixtures for his saloon across the border in Naco, Mexico.[3]

One visible sign of change came in 1915 when the Crystal Palace Saloon was turned into a movie theater named the Crystal Theater. The building was suited perfectly for this as it was renovated with a stage and rows of box seats on each side.[3]

The Crystal Palace has seen many owners and many incarnations. This includes being a ticket office for the Greyhound Bus Station that housed a curio shop and lunch counter. Although the original bar may be lost to time somewhere, a replica was built in 1964 during a major reconstruction effort put on by the Historic Tombstone Adventures (HTA) included the addition of the well-known wallpaper, new flooring, and new furnishings.[3]

DEFINITIONS

Earthbound – a ghost or spirit that was unable to cross over to the other side at the time of death and is stuck in this physical plane. **Entity** – anything that has a separate, distinct existence, though not necessarily material in nature. **Intelligent Haunting** – an interaction on the physical plane as in communication or object movement. **Place-Centered Haunting** – a location where paranormal events frequently take place. **Poltergeist** – non-human entity (noisy ghost) usually more malicious than ghosts or deceased human beings. May involve thumping, banging, levitation or movement of objects, object movement, stone throwing, and starting fires. **Reciprocal Apparition** – a rare type of spirit phenomenon in which both the agent and the percipient are able to see and respond to each other. **Spirit Box** – an electronic device used for direct communication with spirits, which acts as a medium, through the use of radio frequency (also called a ghost box). **Trigger Object** – an object used in order to elicit communication from an entity. The idea is to get the entity to MOVE the trigger object.

ADVENTURE ENTERTAINS GHOST SEEKERS

The company, *Spirit Expeditions,* owned by Dawane Harris, now living in Oregon, got his start in entertaining ghost seeking enthusiasts several years ago when he and his wife, a psychic medium, lived in Tombstone.³ The couple began their ghost hunting adventure at the **Crystal Palace and Saloon Restaurant**. *Ghost Adventures,* a television show, had its cast investigate specific areas of the saloon proclaiming the location to be haunted.⁴

Video footage of a paranormal event that occurred in the basement of the saloon involved a glass bottle flying off of a shelf smashing itself against a wall followed by the sound of footsteps walking away. This video can be viewed on YouTube.com, under the name, "Crystal Palace Ghost Hunt Data of a Bottle Flying Across the Room Smashing Against A Wall" filmed February 21, 2010.⁵

ENCOUNTERS

My husband and I wanted to visit Tombstone, Arizona as part of our multi-city trip out West during the first week in May 2010. As one of our stops, we signed up to participate in a ghost hunting adventure, to take place the eve of our arrival at the Crystal Palace Saloon and Restaurant, located near the infamous Bird Cage saloon. Our means of getting to Tombstone was by renting a car and driving approximately 4 hours through miles and miles of desert. Once we reached Tombstone, we checked into a basic hotel, and prepared ourselves for an evening of intrigue and mystery.

THE TOWN. When we arrived into Tombstone, we noticed the main draw involved a long street consisting of a few blocks with few people wandering about. We would be told by the locals that this little town can often bring huge crowds up to nearly 100,000 during special events. We walked up and down a long street admiring what businesses had remained opened, then proceeding to The Crystal Palace and Saloon for supper and ghost hunt.

GHOST HUNT. Once the ghost experience began, our small group of ten participants were given a few pieces of equipment and were explained how to use the devices. We began by sitting around a television monitor to watch a video segment created by *Ghost Adventures*, a haunted television show with cast, who had just investigated the Crystal Palace location a few years prior. Once the video was finished, it was "lights out" and our investigation began.

POOL TABLE. We initially stood by a pool table located near a large window in front of the saloon. Old time music was played as a trigger object to elicit paranormal activity. Our tour guide, who led the ghost experience, also a psychic medium, attempted to make contact with the ghost residents who frequented the saloon (cowboys and gamblers) by asking questions out loud.

FLASHLIGHT. Her first trigger object was that of a small flashlight. She placed it on a ledge near the window (about 10 feet away from us) and asked the resident ghost(s) to flicker it on and off to her voice commands. When she asked it to flicker, it did.

POOL BALL. The next trigger object was that of a pool ball. She had us crowd in a circle around the pool table. She explained to everyone that one of the "balls" on the table had moved to her voice commands in the past. Unfortunately, on this night, no ball moved and most seemed glued to the table.

CARD TABLE. The next trigger object was that of a deck of cards spread out in "hands" on a poker table. Her attempt was to see if she could arouse any card movement since poker games often led to shoot outs. Unfortunately, on this night, the cards and poker chips did not move or fly off the wooden table.

HALLWAY. Before going into the basement cellar, the tourists gathered in a small hallway just outside of the gaming hall and near the basement cellar door to use our meters to attempt to make contact. This area was reported to be a place where apparitions had appeared in the past. We suspected it was because of its location to the nearby basement door that led down to where the opening of the mine hole was found. We all sat down on the floor in this cramped, darkened hallway (1-2 candles burning for light). We positioned ourselves to be in a semi-circle in order to attempt to make contact with one or more spirits. No contact was made in this area this evening.

QUESTIONS / THOUGHTS

Why am I on a ghost hunting adventure when there appears to be no ghosts? I have a reasonable answer for this – one person is company and ten people are a crowd. Spirits, especially those who might make contact, do not like crowds or a mix of energies. Therefore, it was of no surprise that the resident ghost(s) did not want to "perform" for us in front of numerous adults and few young children. My experience has always been that ghosts will show to one or two people but will rarely to never show to a crowd.

Yes, the place was haunted. Spirits come and go on their own terms and time schedules. The moon phase that evening was a half moon. Due to the environmental conditions, it was possible the energy field was strong enough to elicit activity. However, I felt uncomfortable with young children being on this type of ghost adventure.

BASEMENT CELLAR. At the point we realized we were not going to get much activity in the hallway, we proceeded to … "THE BASEMENT CELLAR." Talk about an unnerving experience. We all walked down some steps through a trap door that led us down a long, narrowed hallway. Once we all arrived safely down the stairs, we stopped a short distance in and observed to our right, an open mining hole that was never sealed shut. The story was that a miner attempted to go down into the hole, lost his footing, and broke his neck causing his death. I believe they left him in this hole as it was too difficult to retrieve his body. As of May 2010, the hole remained opened.

SPIRIT BOX SESSION. If you look at the video on YouTube.com entitled, "Crystal Palace Ghost Hunt Data of a Bottle Flying From a Shelf Across the Room Smashing Against A Wall with Footsteps Walking Away"[4] (filmed February 21, 2010), this is the cramped space we sat in hoping to make contact with the miner. Once we were all seated (lined up against the concrete wall), the host's husband closed the trap door letting us acclimate to sitting in pitch dark conditions. It was at this point that I wanted to run out of there. In fact, I think a few did leave as the darkness was unnerving.

BENCH. In review of the video on YouTube.com, you will see two chairs directly in view situated up against a cinder block cement wall. We (participants) were sitting directly across from these chairs that were lined up all the way down to where the open mine hole was located. With the space being narrow and cramped, what made this experience a little creepy was that I was sitting in the spot where the bottle had flung itself from a shelf smashing against the wall (see video). All items were removed from this area for our safety.

ICE CREAM. The ghost host (psychic) turned on her spirit box (white noise static causing radio frequency bands to capture words) and we all began asking questions to the deceased miner hoping he would share some intelligent words. Two things were apparent during this session: (1) the ghost had a crush on our host extending compliments to her, and (2) the ghost liked specific kinds of ice cream. After our hour long session in the basement cellar, we went back upstairs and the ghost adventure was concluded.

QUESTIONS / THOUGHTS

How reliable are spirit boxes? Spirit boxes scan radio bands very rapidly to convey words from spirits who respond to direct questioning. The spirit we made contact with (miner) through this device was specific in answering our questions. As of this writing, the ghost adventure tour at the Crystal Palace Saloon and Restaurant does not operate anymore as the hosts moved away.

Chapter 24
Dark Shadow

Illustration by Brandy Woods

Chapter 24
Dark Shadow

PHENOMENA

Shadow beings look somewhat different than ghostly phenomena. Whereas ghostly apparitions appear to be a misty white with a vapor-like shape, they are often recognized to have human form. Shadow beings are much darker and have a more shadow-like form. Although shadow beings can have a human outline or shape, because they are dark, their details of appearance can be difficult to make out. The one detail most often noted when seeing a dark shadow being is that they often have glowing red eyes.

The dark countenance and malevolent feelings that are often reported in association with these creatures has led some researchers to speculate that they may be demonic in nature. If they are demons, we wonder what their purpose or intent is in letting themselves be seen in this manner. Is it merely to frighten?

HAUNTED CHURCHES

I grew up believing a church was considered a safe haven, sacred, and a location offering protection for those in need. I also felt if any ghostly entity sought refuge in a church, that the spirit was harmless and wanted a place of everlasting peace.

Historical churches, especially, may be prone to some ghostly haunts. These haunts are generally harmless but remind us that no place is exempt from inhabitants. However, is it possible that some churches may attract negative or demonic energies? The answer, I believe, is "yes."

DEFINITIONS

Agent – a living agent who is the focus of poltergeist activity. **Anomaly** – something that cannot be explained. For example, an orb that is not the result of a camera mishap or caused by external factors such as dust, bugs, moisture, reflections, and gas emissions. **Attack** - feeling weak, low energy, dizzy, sick to stomach, ill, and overcome by strong or rotting smells, such as deceased animals or scents. **Illusion** – a perception between what is perceived and what is reality. **Intelligent Haunting** – an interaction with an entity on the physical plane, including object movement or touching. **Percipient** – a person who sees (perceives) an apparition. **Shadow People** – shadow-like entities most often seen in one's peripheral vision. Differs from ghosts such that recognizable facial features and clothing characteristics are lacking. Very frequently, sightings are accompanied by feelings of dread, menace, or threat. **Touched** – the act of having physical contact from a spirit or entity such as pulling hair, shirt tugging, pushing, etc.

ENCOUNTER

I was a professional wedding photographer from 2009-2013. One of my clients was having her wedding at a church in a less than appealing part of town. I needed to do some preparation work for this wedding so I went to the church to assess its areas, take some pictures, and figure out its lighting issues.

I had been forewarned that this specific church left its doors opened during the day attracting homeless people who liked to sleep in the pews. Not thrilled to hear this, I convinced myself that I had a job to do and to just be careful.

I arrived to the church one early morning. I opened one of two large, heavy doors and walked inside. Nervous, it took me a few minutes to feel comfortable being there alone. It did occur to me while I was standing in the doorway that if I needed to leave quickly, I should have a get-away plan. I saw no homeless people lying in any of the pews.

HEART POUNDING. Even though the church appeared

empty, my nervous system was not feeling comfortable being in there alone. There were moments when my stomach felt knotted, my head started to play mind tricks on me, and my heart fluttered and raced. On several occasions, I turned around to look behind me because I felt as if something was watching me. Paranoid? Perhaps.

At what point do you give credit to your inner voice and listen to it when your nervous system is trying to tell you something?

As I was walking around the inside of the church, I just could not shake this uncomfortable feeling I was having. I needed to go up into the church balcony to take a few pictures. With every step I took walking up the balcony stairs, my heart began racing faster and faster. My balcony experience was uneventful.

MAIN FLOOR. Back on the main floor, I was no more than 15 minutes away from departing the church when something caught my eye from behind my left shoulder. It appeared to be a dark shadow with a slithering motion going into one of the back corner rooms. Curious about what I had just seen, I decided to follow it.

BACK ROOM. I do not know why I felt so brave to follow the dark shadow to a "back room." I felt I needed to figure out the mystery of it. When I arrived to the back corner, I saw a bare room and a window off to the right. My first thought was that the shadow was casted from something outside. This was until I realized there were no trees, objects, clouds, or cars on a road to create shadows. It was at this point that my gut feeling told me to get out of the church.

EVIL ENTITY? I had never known "dark shadows" to be "nice" ghosts. Usually, misting energies are often "white" in appearance. In fact, I grew up believing that anything "dark" was evil and dangerous. I should have worn a cross for protection while in the church. However, my beliefs about churches being sacred as well as my feeling protected by my guardian angels is what kept me strong. I hurried out the door.

TRIPPED AND FALLING. As I attempted to leave the church, I was not more than two steps out the door when I felt something trip my right foot forcing me to fall to one knee, smashing it against a concrete step, while catching my fall by grabbing onto one of the hand rails. While holding the hand rail, I found myself having extreme knee pain. My fear at this point was that I broke something and would not be able to walk to my car. As I looked in front and around me (dazed and injured), it had occurred to me that few people drove down the street outside of the church and that few would probably not stop to help me. I hobbled to my car and drove away. I did not return to the church until the couple's wedding day.

QUESTIONS / THOUGHTS

Was this shadow being a figment of my imagination? Was my falling outside the church caused by my lack of attention to a short step that was poorly positioned beyond the church doors? Or, did something trip me as I exited the building?

This church attracts homeless people who sleep in its pews. On occasion, a homeless person will die and be found lying on a pew. Not knowing the history of deaths that occurred in this church, my question would be, "did an unsettled or angry person die in this church creating a lingering energy?"

Finally, did I have a guardian angel who helped me grab onto the hand rail as I found myself falling down 15 concrete steps? I believe the answer to this question is, "Yes."

Chapter 25
Looking Blue Today

Art Illustration by Brandy Woods

Chapter 25
Looking Blue Today

<u>TOM'S STORY</u>

My name is Tom. I had a pretty good life back in the day. I was a farmer who built my home on the land I inherited from my father. I followed in my father's footsteps by growing crops in the field and raising meat animals to sell at local rendering shops. I had a loving wife and children.

Like others in my area, I tirelessly made my living at farming making it a full-time job often feeling rewarded by its financial payoff. A devoted Christian, my family and I attended church on Sundays socializing with our neighbors during potluck lunch often held in the church basement after the service. In my spare time, I enjoyed the sports of fishing and hunting while collecting pocket knives and enjoying the luxury of wearing fishing hats. I always kept a watchful eye over my family, property, and neighbors. I felt blessed to have it all.

However, what I did not see coming was a turbulent economy that turned our comfortable lifestyle into a disruptive nightmare. A failed stock market affected our family savings losing half of it. Two years of droughts not only limited my crop production but made it difficult for me to repay my debt to the bank. And, my receipt of poor returns on my selling meat animals to rendering shops made my effort to raise animals pointless.

One day, while I was feeling at my lowest, I decided to take a walk to my mailbox. What I discovered waiting for me was a notice of foreclosure from my bank on my property telling me they would be taking the land I inherited from my father to repay my debt.

This was my breaking point. My happy life was too stressful to bear anymore. The biggest blow to my ego was losing my father's land. Three days after receipt of that foreclosure notice, I walked to my barn, climbed up the stairs located just inside the door leading to the hay loft, put a rope around my neck, took my last looks of my home and farm, said a prayer to my wife and children, walked three steps forward out of the hay loft door into space, and died by hanging myself.

They found me later that day hanging forty feet in the air just outside the barn loft. It took three men to bring me down to the ground. My wife and children watched feeling traumatized.

STILL AROUND - ENCOUNTERS

My name is Carol. I visually saw the ghost of Tom several years ago when I was in my late teens. I was at my friend's house (formerly Tom's home) at a gathering playing *Apples to Apples*, a card game. Many of us gathered in my friend's porch so we wouldn't disturb her mother or father who remained in the house.

The house and barn then was approximately 100+ years old. While playing cards, I felt uncomfortable. I glanced at the window in the porch and caught a glimpse of Tom peering at me through it.

Seeing his old, skeletal, gaunt face scared me to death. His blue'ish, translucent look still haunts my mind to this day. He was wearing a floppy fishing hat that had a stripe on the brim.

THE ENCOUNTER. The barn where he hung himself still stands on the property (130 years later). When I saw him, it was probably 9:00 PM.-9:30 PM. It was a rainy evening. There were raindrops on the window. Due to the time of year, there was just enough light outside for me to be able to see right through him. I noticed the clouds passing behind him.

SHOCKED. My heart pounded from the fright of seeing him. I began to sweat. I couldn't breathe I was so scared. I froze in my chair in fear as he watched me from outside the window peering in at me and my friends.

5 SECONDS. Tom looked at me for about 5 seconds and then, he vanished. It was at this point that I asked my friend if her Dad was outside walking around the house. She said he was in bed sleeping.

HALLWAY. I needed to confirm that her Dad was in bed so I took a walk down a hallway leading to his bedroom. As I walked closer to his room, I could hear him snoring. Was this incident my imagination? Who did I see in the window?

CONFIRMATION. When I returned to the card game, I asked others if they had seen a translucent, blue'ish faced man peering in the window. Since all of party attenders were drunk, except me, no one had noticed Tom but me.

<u>CONFIRMATION OF TOM</u>

My friend had known about Tom for years. He had been making himself known to all her family around the house with noises and object movement. With such a strong attachment to the farm property and feeling at a loss for losing his father's farm, it didn't surprise me that he would want to hang around to watch over it. He probably felt it was his duty to keep watch over what his father had entrusted to him. With his wife and children long gone, to date, Tom remains protective over the property.

OCCURRENCES

Here are some of the unusual occurrences that kept Tom noticed on my friend's family farm. Even after death, he felt compelled to watch over his father's land:

1. Tom liked to take and hide the Dad's fishing hats.
2. Tom liked to take and hide the Dad's pocket knives.
3. Tom liked to make noises in the house.
4. Tom's footsteps could be heard walking down the hallway.
5. Tom would be spotted in the attic several times (gray misty image).
6. When I stayed overnight and shared a bed with my friend, Tom would rock the bed until I told him to stop.
7. Tom was helpful. For example, when my friend was in the basement doing laundry, there was a time when the cap of the detergent bottle accidentally fell off and rolled behind the washing machine where it could not be reached. A day or so later, the cap would be placed on top of the washing machine.

Chapter 26
C-R-E-E-E-K

Art Illustration by Katie Wheeler

Chapter 26
C-R-E-E-E-K

ENTERING A VACANT HOUSE

My name is Brenda. "My grandmother, who passed away in 2007 at the age of 96, was the last of my paternal grandparents. Months after we buried her, the house stood still and quiet with all their things (grandfather and grandmother) in their places as if they were awaiting their return.

"I felt compelled to go over to their country home to begin the daunting task of sorting through their stuff to put into storage. It was my hope to clear the home of its treasures before intruders realized it was abandoned.

"As I drove to their home, located in the middle of rural America, memories of what it was like when visiting them crossed my mind. As I arrived onto the property, the reality hit me that only an empty house stood vacant with no one to care for it. Chills went up my spine. I got out of my car, looked around, and noticed an aged outhouse, collapsed garage, dying trees, barn, and a 105+ year old Colonial house. The barn and home were built by my great grandfather in the mid- to late 1800's - definitely standing the test of time. Few family members knew I was there that day with the intention to pack up their things.

"For the past several years, this Colonial home had seen a few repairs. I begin to wonder if there were any hidden secrets to be found in the house. I guess I was just about to find out.

"As I approached the home, I noticed a sign nailed to the right side of the porch upon entrance into the building next to its screened door, "NO TRESPASSING." The entire place looked worn and tired, falling to pieces. I began to feel uneasy about my venturing there. As I tried to open the main door to go inside the house, it felt as though someone or something was holding me back not allowing me to go in. It was as if something didn't want me to enter. Not believing the place was haunted, I gave the door a shove and it opened right up.

"Before pushing the main door open, I noticed two ears of corn hanging on the wall (used for decoration), a fly swatter (hanging on the same nail), and two folding chairs that leaned up against the wall. A thin piece of paneling served to cover a large hole in the porch floor as you entered. The hole underneath led directly to the basement. The floor panel was rotting.

"As I turned the antique door handle and pushed the main door open, I heard, "s-q-u-e-e-k" ..."s-q-u-e-e-k" ... it did occur to me that the door springs needed some oil lubrication. Being careful to walk over the rotting panel floor, I stepped over it and proceeded to go inside the house. *What an eerie feeling.* Memories began to surface in my mind of those few times I had been in the home as a child. As I viewed an old antique stove that remained in the same spot for nearly 100 years, I noticed the paint on it was peeling back due to its age, lack of care, and weather elements. A mouse nest was found just inside the baking door area where my grandmother's famous baked beans were once heated. She was an awesome cook. You could feel a sense of life remaining in this house, though vacant.

"As I walked into the house I said, *Hello, is anyone in here*? I was praying no one would answer me back. My being there alone made me feel somewhat uncomfortable. Before I went upstairs to the second floor, I checked all the rooms on the first floor making sure there were no surprises around any corner. Inside the kitchen, to my right, I noticed a broken glass window, probably broken because of a fallen tree limb during a storm or bird that flew into it. Shattered glass was all over the kitchen floor near that window. I was careful to walk past certain areas in the house as black mold started growing in places where there were water leaks – such as in the livingroom on its walls, my grandmother's sewing area, and the small washroom just inside the kitchen. To the right of the antique stove were stairs that led up to the second floor. I took a deep breath and began walking up the narrow, mahogany colored stairs carrying a few plastic bins."

THE ENCOUNTER

"With every step I took to walk up those stairs ... I heard a continuous c-r-e-e-k ... c-r-e-e-k ... snap! The stairs were narrow with drywall pieces from the walls and ceiling all over them. The drywall pieces were crumbled making the steps slippery. The sounds I heard as I made my way up those stairs affected every nerve in my body. My heart began beating faster. My breathing felt labored. I was sweating from anxiety. As I looked up toward the second floor, I saw the door leading into the guest bedroom half open. This gave me the willies. I had wondered if a draft had closed it part way over time or if something were behind the door.

My goal was to get up to the second floor without falling down the stairs. I began to wonder how my grandparents managed to climb up those stairs back in the day.

"As I reached the second-floor landing, I decided to look inside the guest bedroom first to make sure there were no surprises awaiting me. As I pushed the door fully open, I cautiously looked inside. Nothing. Just wallpaper falling off its walls and some plaster from the ceiling lying on the floor. I walked out of that room and went down the short hallway, checking each of the two rooms that existed down the hall. First, the master bedroom, to the right. I had noticed aged newspapers were used as curtains hanging down from each window. I went over to see if I could check their date and I believe they said a month in the 1970's or 80's. That's a long time to be taped to a window. A small bedroom on the other side once my father's room, and previous to him, my deceased great aunt, Lilly, who passed away as a young child in the early 1900's. A single bed remained in that room used as a storage area for boxes and boxes of outdated commodity items, such as cereal and personal products. It had appeared to me that the mice had gotten into a few of those things leaving their droppings as payment.

"I was now ready to tackle bundling up items from the spare junk room that was down the hallway. Years ago, as a child, my grandmother would tell me to never go into that room. A curtain was used as its door. What was in that room that was so important? I just remember how stern she was about my not going in there. So, years later, with no guard around, I flung open the curtain and went into it. Hmmm … no surprises so far.

"What I saw in that room were piles and piles of papers along with several unused items given to my grandparents for many Christmases. My grandparents never believed in using electrical items, such as toasters or heating blankets. I think they thought the items would catch on fire.

"Although the house had electrical power, I decided to not waste electricity and keep the lights off. I was probably in that room for no more than an hour when I heard footsteps echo from downstairs. Thinking it was my mother, I called down and said, "*I'm up here*." No answer. An odd feeling came over me. "*Hello, anyone down there?*" No answer. My heart started beating and my pulse felt faint. Someone was in this house and I was trapped upstairs in this room. Was there an intruder? I felt so trapped that I snuck into the next room (because it had a door), closed it gently, and barricaded myself into a corner behind a lot of tall things. Minutes felt like hours. Footsteps continued. Then I heard ... "C-r-e-e-k .... C-r-e-e-k ... the door to the basement. It was at this point that I decided to get out of that house before the person decided to come back up from the basement. I got up, crept quietly down the steps, and made a run for it.

"As I made my way to the bottom of the stairs, I peeked around the corner into the kitchen. I noticed the front door remained in the exact position it was when I went upstairs. As I crept through the kitchen, I could smell a strong scent of a man's cologne. I stood still for just a moment to listen to any sounds I could hear around me. As I turned and looked at the basement door, I noticed that it remained in a closed position. Funny, the door sounded as if it had been opened but ... it hadn't been opened.

The smell of the cologne reminded me of a popular brand my grandfather use to wear. It was called, "*Old Spice*." Is it possible that my grandfather or my great grandfather

Chapter 27
Artwork Not For Sale

Art Illustration by Katie Wheeler

was checking on things in the house?

"My mind began racing. Since I didn't believe at first that the house was haunted, my mind suddenly turned to IT IS HAUNTED. I didn't really have a logical explanation for all the sounds. The front door remained untouched. The basement door was closed. I smelled a strong scent of men's cologne in the kitchen. *Who was here or was there anyone ever here?* Pondering no further, I rushed out of the house and stood on the lawn calling my mother. With my voice trembling, I had asked she come over right away and to bring extra garbage bags. We went back into the house together. I never went into that house alone again."

GHOSTLY SMELLS AND SOUNDS

Both doors leading inside the house and down into the basement showed no sign of entry. The smell of men's cologne, especially the scent my grandfather or his father worn after shaving, drifted toward me as if he were standing right next to me. Ghosts do have a tendency to let people know they are around. Scents, doors opening and closing, slamming, footsteps, object movement, etc. are nothing more than signs that a former presence or ghostly intruder is near. If a ghost wants to scare or startle someone, they will use what they have to cause a reaction. Mission accomplished.

Chapter 27
Artwork Not For Sale

PHENOMENA

"This is a beautiful piece of artwork, Katie," I said. "Thanks, I like painting ladybugs and this one turned out really good," she replies. "How much do you want for it?" I ask. "Oh, it is not for sale. I don't think I could part with this one. I think I'm going to hold onto it for a long time," she replies.

Personal possessions and artwork can often retain levels of energy from its owners. In some cases, the energy may be minimal. In other cases, the intensity of emotion inflicted toward or about something may be strong. Owners that have strong, personal attachments to their things and properties may be reluctant in allowing, even in death, to let their land or possessions fall into the hands of new owners. Some people go to extremes in cursing or placing spells on their possessions to ward off owners.

BACKGROUND OF PAINTING "CRYING BOY"

In a 2016 haunted television episode called "*Deadly Possessions*," as narrated by its creator and museum owner, Zak Bagans, he demonstrates how curses can haunt the owning of beautiful pieces of artwork leading to dangerous and/or deadly conditions. The artwork (original or reproduction), entitled "*Crying Boy*," was brought directly to Zak Bagan's museum located in Las

Vegas, Nevada in late 2015 or early 2016 by a young woman who resided in England and had been its caretaker for several years. She decided she did not want to take care of the painting any longer as it scared her. She asked Zak Bagans, owner of the *Deadly Possessions* haunted museum to adopt the painting giving him ownership. With hesitation, he accepted the artwork. This artwork and its reproductions were known to start deadly fires in homes when hung on a wall. The woman had purchased it from an art peddler on a street in England.

Painting of *The Crying Boy*
Artist Bruno Amadio

WHAT IS KNOWN ABOUT "CRYING BOY"

According to information submitted to Wikipedia, *The Crying Boy* artwork piece was a mass-produced print of a painting by Italian painter Bruno Amadio, also known as Giovanni Bragolin. The artwork piece was widely distributed from the 1950s onwards. There are numerous versions with all portraits of a tearful young boy or girl. Widely known, certain urban legend attributes that a "curse" was placed on the painting.

According to a British tabloid newspaper, *The Sun*, on September 4, 1985, it reported that a firefighter from Princes Road, Essex, Chelmsford, England was claiming that undamaged copies of the painting were frequently found amidst the ruins of burned houses. He stated no firefighter would allow a copy of the painting into his own house. Over the next few months, *The Sun* and other tabloids ran several articles on house fires suffered by people who had owned the painting.

By the end of November 1985, belief in the painting's curse was widespread enough that *The Sun* was organizing mass bonfires of the paintings, sent in by readers. Steve Punt investigated the curse of *The Crying Boy* painting and concluded that in testing its prints, they were treated with a varnish containing fire repellent and that a string holding the painting to the wall would be the first to burn away resulting in the painting to land face down on the floor and thus be protected. No explanation otherwise.

Chapter 28
Guardian Angel? Uh, No.

Photograph by Kelly Schutz

Does This Look Like a Guardian Angel to You?

Chapter 28
Guardian Angel? Uh, No.

PHENOMENA

"This doll was my guardian angel" ... she said ... as it was taken away never to be seen again. I can hardly imagine a doll who mysteriously shows up on a property during an intense clean-up (face up in the dirt) would "not want" to be found. In fact, as I have been writing this section, the picture keeps turning itself upside down and backwards. The first time I have ever seen an image turn itself on its own without my effort.

THE STORY

I have seen first-hand how negative energies can destroy a family. In fact, if given enough emotional charge, negative energies can single people out and attempt to destroy their lives one by one. This doll may look innocent to you but it's far from. Perhaps a little worn from the outdoor elements. It has a dark side – one that cannot be denied. No younger family member of mine (4 girls), including myself, can recall having this doll growing up. The doll showed "face up" in the dirt in the backyard when demolition of several buildings was taking place. It wanted to be found. Call it my imagination but I never had a good feeling about white plastic skin or white-gray-haired baby dolls with piercing blue eyes. Judgmental?

WHEN THIS ALL BEGAN

Several months ago, my mother began the painstaking process of opening three sheds in the backyard that were held under lock and key by my father who stuffed all of them with things from garage sales and auctions. My father had a hoarding disorder and would not allow anyone to look at or touch his stuff. Upon his death, my mother took access of the sheds and began eliminating his things. As part of her elimination process, she made the decision to allow the children to sort through and select items prior to her putting the rest on an estate auction.

A few months before the auction while clearing rubbish in the backyard, this doll was discovered face up in the ground with its body covered by dirt. No one had noticed this doll before. It suddenly appeared. In fact, no one really knew where it came from. Most suspected it was a doll picked up by my father at one of his auctions. Another theory was that it was a doll my siblings played with growing up. However, no child recalled ever seeing or playing with this doll. It was obvious this doll had been in the ground for several years as its face was discolored to a pale white, its eyes were washed out to a deep piercing blue, and its hair was bleached to a chalky white-gray. It is a bit frightening to look at due to common familiarity.

The find of this doll led to a series of jokes by some family members who took it upon themselves to move it around the yard to various places, tying it to a post, and turning it upside down on a burn pile. The doll had been thrown away three times in a large dumpster only to find it returned to its usual position by one of the sheds. As a believer in negative forces, watching this doll become the butt of jokes and tormented with acts of stupid was too much for me to endure. After all, the number one haunted item reported on the planet is ... a doll.

Being annoyed by the continuous acts of doll treatment, I took it upon myself to pick up the doll lying by the shed and toss it deep down into the dumpster. I threw the doll so far down that it would be impossible to retrieve it without some leg work to get it out. Within a week after tossing it, the doll would be upright in the exact spot where I had taken it away. I recalled telling my family members ... "leave this doll alone" ... "you have no idea how haunted this thing is." Being laughed at, all I hoped for was that the doll would be taken away never to be seen again. One week later, the doll would be sitting right next to the shed in its usual location. No one would admit to retrieving the doll from the dumpster (which would have been a chore based on how far I threw it down inside).

Knowing the dangers of touching it ... I had no choice if I wanted to rid it. On its final day at the property, I decided to put on some gloves, take a garbage bag, say a prayer, pick it up, say another prayer, and wrap it gently in the bag. I put the doll in my car and drove it 125 miles away to a dumpster located behind a restaurant. I said a prayer, asked it to not follow me, and threw it inside the smelly unit. I would be mad too if my resting place was a mess of smelly and rotten restaurant waste.

A few days later, my mother told me this doll was her guardian angel. I thought to myself, "what an odd thing to say." My mother told me since I took the doll off the property that despair had been thrust upon her and family members. I told her the doll had negative forces attached to it and that it had to be removed. Typical reaction of someone under its influences.

Like clockwork, as each day ticked by after its removal … one day later … my brother's dog was hit on the road and had to be put down … two days later … I discovered I had cancer (with no family history of this type of condition) … three days later … my sister's daughter's car wrecks on the highway … four days later … my brother-in-law's father passes away unexpectedly. With all these events happening, my mother says most sincerely, "I miss the doll, it was my guardian angel."

A doll perceived to be a guardian angel … yet treated as the butt of jokes. Maybe the doll liked the attention. After all, it had been ignored for years … lying in the ground. Found and given lots of play time. Probably missed that too. Simply stated, were these acts of devastation coincidences or acts of a rebellious nature by the doll?

Believer or skeptic ... after a week of being removed ... negative forces continued until the auction came and went. The auction appeared to be a success. Would having this doll on the premises during the auction make any difference at all? Cannot be verified.

I have heard of dolls claimed to be haunted placed behind glass ... yet having the ability to get out of their displays and crawl across the floor. Zak Bagans has a large doll display (haunted dolls) in his Las Vegas haunted museum. Some of the most dangerous dolls on this earth are located in his museum, in England, and on an isolated island. Those who are prone to illness, like schizophrenia, have tendencies to imprint their energies onto an object.

This story is not meant to scare people away from the ownership of having a doll. Although seeing the picture flip upside down before I finish writing this story tends to bother me some. No one can put their finger on who owned this doll. That alone is enough reason to rid it.

Removing this doll from the property (where it probably felt happiest) was a huge risk for me. As you learned, a cancer diagnosis came shortly after along with others having a string of negative events. Call these events coincidental. Claim these events to be of their time. Do I think this doll had anything to do with my illness? I think the timing of it along with no family history of this type of cancer makes me wonder "a little."

Chapter 29
Cowboy in the Cabin Window

Artistic Illustration – By Kelly Renee Schutz

Hill City, near Deadwood, South Dakota

Chapter 29
Cowboy in the Cabin Window

PHENOMENA

On a steep hill just outside of Hill City, South Dakota, lies a cabin. Located nearly 30-40 miles from Deadwood, SD and 70 miles from Dewey, SD, this cabin resides on what is referred to as "the southern hills." Little do most cabin visitors realize, a cowboy, who may have been a cattle rancher or miner in this area, is patiently waiting for their arrival. Reports of feeling watched, unexplained infestation of flies, eerie elk rug, and moments of discomfort disrupt peacefulness while keeping the most sensitive on high alert.

ACTUAL PICTURE OF CABIN

Photo Taken by Brandy Woods of "The Western Star"

HISTORY OF HILL CITY, SOUTH DAKOTA

According to a general history written on Wikipedia (2016), Hill City, South Dakota has its roots in the Black Hills mining rush as of the late 19th century. Tin mining was dominant in the 1880s and led to an influx of capital and people into the area. As the mining industry subsequently waned, tourism and timber became increasingly important to the area. The discovery of gold opened the Black Hills, and the Hill City area, to mining. Hill City was first settled by miners in 1876, who referred to the area as Hillyo. This was the second American settlement in the Black Hills. Hill City is the oldest city still in existence in Pennington County. A post office was constructed and opened on November 26, 1877. The city almost became a ghost town when miners relocated to the northern Black Hills after the discovery of gold there.

In 1883, tin was discovered near Hill City, and the population rebounded. The Harney Peak Tin Mining, Milling, and Manufacturing Company made its headquarters on Main Street. The company was backed by English financiers and bought 1,100 prospecting sites around the area. As mining grew, the city became known for its wild living and was once referred to as "a town with a church on each end and a mile of Hell in between." At one time, 15 saloons were located on Main Street. The company built the Harney Peak Hotel on Main Street to entertain its management and executives. Upon realizing the tin market was unsustainable, the company ceased operation in 1902. Within a forty to seventy-mile radius around Hill City, were cabins surrounded by large sections of land. Cattle ranchers used the railroad to load their livestock onto cars sending them to Deadwood, South Dakota. Cattle ranchers and miners dominated the southern hills region.

COWBOY IN THE WINDOW

The photo of the cowboy (previous and next pages) was taken on August 10, 2015 at 9:25 AM. Temperature outside was approximately 60 degrees. A small stream, located 2-3 feet from where this image was taken, glistened as it rushed past the cabin. There appeared to be no cemetery in the area. Upon their arrival, Brandy and mother sprayed liquid sage into the air in the cabin to cleanse it (comparable to holy water). Windows were not dirty and the sage cleansing left no residue on anything. They did have issues with flies inside the cabin that never seemed to go away. No odd smells, garbage, or deceased animals that they recalled. During the day, they felt nothing unusual. During the evening, Brandy felt so paranoid about sleeping in the master bedroom with the elk rug that she decided to sleep in another room with her mother. Brandy propped a chair in front of the bathroom door for fear it would open into their room. Cowboy image showed the next morning.

IMAGE INSIDE THE KITCHEN

The arrow is pointing to the window in the kitchen where the cowboy was standing. If you look at the original cabin a few pages prior, the image of the cowboy IS showing. Brandy and her mother felt the cabin was peaceful despite their anxieties about being there.

"THE WESTERN STAR" CABIN

The Western Star, the name of the cabin they stayed in during their time on the guest ranch, resides just outside of Hill City, South Dakota. They rented the cabin during the month of August 2015. It was advertised to be a peaceful get-away.

Known as a guest ranch in the Black Hills of South Dakota, she and her mother booked several nights there. Both being sensitive, they were not anticipating any ghostly activity on their trip. However, they both felt a general 'unease' inside the cabin which only occurred during the evening hours. They felt the unease was worse in the master bedroom which adjoined to the only bathroom. The bathroom had two doors with no locks.

ENLARGED COWBOY IN WINDOW

Photo Enlarged to Show Cowboy in Window
Image is Real, Not Fake - Taken by Brandy Woods
Approximately 100 Filters Were Applied to Debunk

Paranoia of feeling watched caused Brandy to put a chair in front of one of the bathroom doors since it opened into the master bedroom. There was a rug in the master bedroom with an embroidered elk on the floor that gave the impression it was screaming. Brandy felt the master bedroom felt too creepy to stay in so she stayed in a different room with her mother. At night, both left the lights on in a few rooms because of a nagging sense that someone or something was in the cabin with them.

Although they didn't HEAR or SEE anything, there was a definite feeling of unease that surrounded them. Even in the loft bedrooms that resided over the master bedroom, they would often sleep in front of the TV. They didn't notice any orbs but did see some FACES all over the ranch. Of course, this may have been a result of mind matrixing (creating faces within our minds) but that certainly didn't account for everything else they had felt there. Who is the cowboy? Were they being watched? YES.

The ongoing issue with flies brings forth interest. It is noted by investigators that swarms of flies can indicate a deceased presence. Especially when there is no logical explanation. Could the sage burning smell been an attractor? Is it possible or likely that deceased animals lying in the weeds (no matter how small) bring near a swarm of flies? Stuff to consider.

Chapter 30
Haunted Las Vegas Hotels

Illustration – Photo Taken by Kelly Renee Schutz

Las Vegas, Nevada

Chapter 30
Haunted Las Vegas Hotels

PHENOMENA

It has been reported by researchers that Las Vegas could well be the suicide capital of America, perhaps even the world, with many deaths occurring in unsuspecting hotels and surrounding area. According to Michelle Trudeau, who wrote the article entitled, *Las Vegas: The Suicide Capital of America*, dated December 10, 2008, states that in Las Vegas, the odds of dying by suicide are strikingly high with residents and visitors alike. Reason unknown – just an odd attraction to wanting to be there. In fact, in a study published in the journal of *Social Sciences and Medicine*, the odds are twice as high as in the rest of the country. In retrospect, Las Vegas, historically, has a suicide rate of about <u>one suicide per day</u>.

REPORTS OF ALLEGED HAUNTINGS
These Hauntings Were Reported by Our Tour Guide

Westgate Las Vegas Hotel (formerly known as the Las Vegas Hilton Hotel and before that, International Hotel). It has been reported that Elvis, famous singer and actor, still remains there. He had performed to more than 2.5 million fans at the International-Las Vegas Hilton from July 1969 to 1977 (death). Barry Manilow, well-known singer of the

1970's and beyond, who was contracted to perform at the Las Vegas Hilton for years, stayed on the secluded, top floor of the hotel, as did Elvis. Manilow had commented on PBS television show (2015) when promoting the purchase of his music that he had seen Elvis roaming the top floor of the Las Vegas Hilton when he stayed there. Many people allege to see, hear, and sense Elvis in several locations within the hotel, including the showroom.

Redd Foxx's Former Home. The former Redd Foxx's home is located on Eastern Avenue, near Hacienda Avenue. Redd Foxx, who starred in the television series, "Sanford and Sons," once lived in the building, formerly his home, where Shannon Day Realty is or was located, in the mid-1990's, early 2000's (could still be there as of this writing). Speculation remains that Foxx still haunts the building because he was angry that he lost the property due to back taxes. He had owed approximately $1 million dollars in taxes when the IRS foreclosed upon the homes and his personal effects to repay the debt.

It was mentioned during the haunted tour that on occasion, loud pool parties can be heard behind the house, even though the pool has remained drained and dry for several years. Some objects inside the home have moved (pranks). During other times, objects have flung across the room, a sign of his moodiness.

Stratosphere Casino and Hotel. A young man is often seen going up the escalator within the casino area around midnight to 2:00 AM to residually prepare himself to jump off one of the top floors that has access to the outside by falling. The man fell through a McDonalds restaurant below landing inside. A residual haunting means a continuous playback of the incident.

Riviera Casino and Hotel. The historic and what was one of few existing casinos of age, closed to the public in May 2015. It had been televised and reported by *Ghost Adventures*, a haunted television show that a young woman took her life by jumping off one of the highest floors in the building from a balcony landing onto the concrete slab below. It was reported she bounced about 6 feet into the air before succumbing to her death. Her spirit was reported to have been seen or heard. The *Ghost Adventures* team went into the building just after the incident to determine how haunted the casino hotel was as more than one suicide occurred there.

REPORTED BY SHADOWLANDS PARANORMAL WEBSITE
These casinos are just "some" reported to be haunted.

Bellagio Casino and Hotel (formerly the Dunes Hotel and Casino) – in 1993, before the closing and implosion of the Dunes, cold spots were reported throughout many of its main areas and towers. After hours, on the top floor in a lounge area, a blue glow was seen and voices of people heard, when no one was around. It is unknown if the hauntings continue since new construction of the Bellagio sits in its very spot.

Caesar's Palace Hotel Casino. On a graveyard shift, a cocktail waitress went into the ladies' room, just down the escalator in the Forum Casino, and noticed the faucets were turning on and off by themselves. When she went to put her hands underneath one of them, it had stopped. She was in the restroom alone.

Circus Circus. Perhaps the oldest casino that remains on the Strip as of this writing. Loud cries for help have been heard in the poker room. In the bathrooms at night, in Rooms 123, 230, 576, and 203, screams of bloody murder can be heard. A 76-year old man who had worked at this casino for nearly 20 years stated 3 people were killed in the kitchen on the same night. A lady who stayed in Room 123 shot herself and her little boys' brains out. They are reported to be haunting the place looking for her husband/his father. A curse that if anyone with the name of the father, Robert, who has black hair, is murdered and hung from the ceiling.

The Excalibur. On the 10th floor, as you walk down the hallway, it feels as though someone is following you, hovering around you, and then, whispers into your ear.

Flamingo Hotel & Casino. This landmark building, one of the oldest, if not the oldest that remains on the Strip as of this writing, is haunted by its founding father, Bugsy Segal. A memorial tombstone commemorating him is found in the back by the pool area. Late at night, people have reported seeing his apparition there. A cleaning lady quit after seeing him on the fifth floor. His mistress, [forgot name], is also reported to be hanging there with him.

Luxor Hotel and Casino. Incident #1. Two construction workers, while building the Pyramid, are reported to have died during its construction. Due to the circumstances surrounding their death and difficulty of the retrieval of their dead bodies, they were entombed within the concrete that supports the building. It has been reported on more than one occasion that during the boat ride that people could take to entertain themselves within the building, bringing them through a tunnel intended to be calming and romantic, that some would feel their shoulders being tapped or brushed up against while in their moving boat. It is unknown if the boat ride remains active to date.

Incident #2. A young woman haunts a portion of the building, especially the first four floors, where she had jumped to her death from a balcony landing on top of buffet food stations in a restaurant. She follows people down hallways.

MGM Grand Hotel and Casino. During the last shift (12:00 AM-8:00 AM), it was reported a figure of a body [indentation] was seen lying on someone's bed. Most women who clean the rooms in the Emerald Tower hold rosary beads as they walk the hallways.

The Mirage. It is reported that the bathrooms by Danny Gan's theatre showroom are haunted. The automatic faucets in those restrooms go on and off without explanation. These occurrences happen late at night and when in the bathroom alone. A cleaning lady holds her rosary as she passes the area. It is rumored that a wall fell down on construction workers when the building was being constructed.

Sun Coast. Several reports of hearing footsteps in one of the bathroom stalls. The faucet, assumed to not be automatic, would turn on by itself.

Tropicana Hotel and Casino. It is not known if this object exists at the entrance as the face of the building had a makeover within the past 10 years of this writing. Up until this time, when visitors would enter the Tropicana building, they would notice a large Tiki mask face and would touch it. They would report thereafter getting a terrible purple rash on their hands, arms, body. Those taking pictures in front of this mask reported a strange purple haze or smoke-like haze in their pictures after development.

REPORTED BY NEWS REPORTER

M Resort. Henry Brean, news reporter for the Las Vegas Review-Journal posted an article online dated April 6, 2015 describing the details about a local man who put a gun to his head and killed himself within the M Resort buffet on Easter due to being banned from it. Just prior to his death, the man filled a box full of complaints and cursed several women he believed wrong him who worked at the buffet that he had showered with gifts and unwanted attention (since September 2010).

In his final, angry message to the world, according to Brean, the man, John Noble, blamed his suicide on depression that set in after the M Resort awarded him free meals at the buffet for life and then banned him from the property in 2013 for harassing some of the women working there. While he was in the buffet area preparing to kill himself, the firefighters were in the parking resort's garage extinguishing a car fire, discovered to be his vehicle.

One month prior to his committing suicide, his mother had passed away. Three weeks prior, he was completely banned from the resort. Read the entire story on the Internet.

Mental health experts say high-profile, public suicides like this are rare and troubling, because they often receive media coverage that can glamourize self-destructive behavior and lead to copycat deaths. The remaining question is, with this man being so angry in his final days at M resort, will his soul remain there cursing those he felt wronged him?

GHOSTLY EXPERIENCE ON THE STRIP

Let me add a disclaimer here. All haunted accounts are alleged until debunked. I travel to Las Vegas at least 2-3 times a year for various reasons and have done so since early 1980's. In the late 1990's, I worked in a casino in Minnesota and came to understand why casino hotels are a draw and targeted by some to be their destination in life. Las Vegas, in my opinion, has the right environmental elements surrounding it. These earthly elements absorb a vast amount of never-ending energy thus allowing the deceased to manifest in ways more difficult to do so in other places.

I have had more than one haunted experience while vacationing in Las Vegas. Being a paranormal investigator, who also attracts ghosts to me, my experiences have not been harmful. If you are an open soul, ghosts will seek out your attention. If you are a closed soul, ghosts will make themselves known when you least expect it.

Wynn/Encore Casino. My ghostly experience occurred when I stayed at the Wynn hotel late November 2015. I don't think you can go anywhere in the Las Vegas area and NOT experience a ghostly moment. New or old building – doesn't matter. The environmental conditions are always right in the Las Vegas area for manifestations. Most people are usually too drunk to notice hauntings that may be around them.

My mission when I go to Las Vegas is to write. Yes, that's what I do. I hide out in a room (sounds boring, huh) and I write. I have done most activities in Las Vegas for the past 30 years, and so, it is easy for me to focus on my projects. Being a ghost investigator is secondary to me, especially since my equipment in finding ghosts is simply "myself."

I love Las Vegas. When I go, I usually stay at the Wynn/Encore Casino Hotels. I have been fortunate to receive free rooms for my being a frequent visitor. This ghostly incident occurred in my Wynn room. I stay at the Encore but no rooms were available during that stay.

There is a lot of truth about being nearly asleep when ghost moments occur. From what I recall, I was almost asleep in my Wynn room (first of three evenings) when something startled me. My room was located on the 60+ something floor, near an elevator. I recall looking up and seeing one floor above me. Any sounds heard were usually passed off as outside hallway noises. I had heard a sound and decided to get up and look out the window. As I looked out, I noticed a bright moon. I thought it looked intriguing.

It was probably 12:30 AM when I lied down to go to sleep. Lights off, "Ahhhh." Within 15 minutes (almost asleep), I had heard 2 knocks directly behind my head on my wall. Thank god it wasn't 3 knocks or I would have been out of there (indicates a demonic presence). It just so happens that my bathroom was directly behind my bedroom wall where my toilet resided. Ghosts like water sources. Where did these knocks come from? Who was knocking on my wall?

I leaned over and attempted to turn on my lights. The light switch system, located on a keypad, was a cool gadget. This keypad could operate the opening and closing of the drapes and lights in all rooms. As I touched the buttons (as I have done so many times), I discovered that nothing was working. Sitting up nervously in a pitch dark room by myself not able to get a light source to turn on was a little nerve wracking.

Something felt odd in this room. I no sooner than got the lights on that the lights underneath my vanity dresser (near my bed), started flickering "on-off" "on-off"... a smooth motion, not quick flicker. Flickering usually indicates an electrical issue. Smooth movement of "on-off" usually indicates a ghost presence. After seeing that, I knew I wasn't alone in my room. Something either followed me to my room or died in this room or general area on that floor. The ghost had its fun with me for about 20 minutes and then left. It did not return the next two nights and the lights functioned properly without issue.

Not all who commit murder or suicide are reported in the newspapers in Las Vegas. This is understandable. I would be curious to learn if someone committed suicide in my room, on that floor, in that building in general, or simply followed me from "somewhere" to that hotel.

Chapter 31
Prince Rupert Hotel–Cycling Mirror

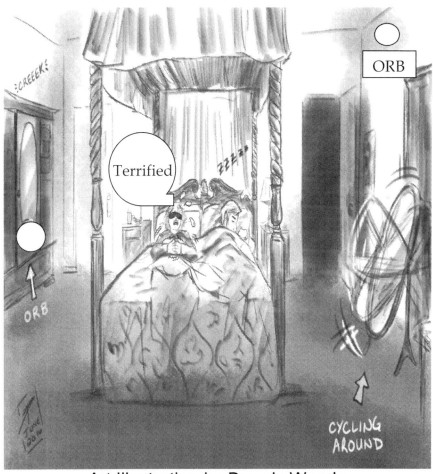

Art Illustration by Brandy Woods
Frightfully True Story As Experienced by Author

Prince Rupert Hotel, Shrewsbury, England

Chapter 31
Prince Rupert Hotel–Cycling Mirror

BRIEF HISTORY

Some historical information about the Prince Rupert Hotel will begin this chapter. A more thorough background can be viewed on the Internet, YouTube, and from a book written by Martin Wood entitled, "Haunted Shrewsbury." The focus of this chapter will be on the reported hauntings at this hotel as well as my own terrifying experience when my husband and I stayed in the Prince Rupert Suite "one" night on May 27, 2016. Would we go back? Only if I were really drunk.

As written in "Haunted Shrewsbury" by Martin Wood, The Prince Rupert Hotel is probably the most haunted hotel in Shrewsbury. The current structure contains parts of homes that range as early as the 1700's. The building dates to approximately the year 1150. Over time, it has experienced the energies of different owners, staff, children, and a variety of personalities.

Named after King Charles I's nephew, Prince Rupert moved to Shrewsbury in 1644 as commander-in-chief of His Majesty's Army and set up his quarters in Jone's Mansion. Jones was an important lawyer in town and the size of his house was testament to his authority.

Mike Matthews, who took over ownership of the hotel in 1996, shares his own haunted experiences on a YouTube video entitled, *Great British Ghosts – The Prince Rupert Hotel, Shrewsbury,* dated September 19, 2012. In this video, he is giving a tour of some of the most haunted rooms to Michaela Strachan, a news reporter, from the Shropshire Star. Together, they walk the hallways, visit rooms, and discuss haunted occurrences. Michaela Strachan is then guided by Martin Wood, local historian, to go down into the cellar where he himself, has been witness to and has had more than one personal haunted experience with an angry gent. See YouTube video link:
https://www.youtube.com/watch?v=TWxN0MYrT3U

YOUTUBE VIDEO

I was particularly happy to notice that when they filmed this YouTube video clip in 2012, that they went directly into the room where we stayed, "The Prince Rupert Suite." Take a moment to notice the location of the MIRROR. Close to wall by the window.

LOOK WHERE THE MIRROR IS NOW

Look at the image below to see where the MIRROR is positioned when my husband and I stayed in this room on May 27, 2016. It is on the other side of the room, in front of an exit door, right next to the bathroom. You will notice that we propped a luggage rack in front of the bathroom door. It was reported that the door would SLAM shut. I wasn't in the mood for slamming, so we attempted to make the effort more difficult.

However, what we didn't realize was the ghostly entity decided to make its presence known by moving and CYCLING THE MIRROR instead. FULL CYCLE. I can see how difficult it would be to CYCLE itself against the wall/window where it had been originally positioned in 2012.

However, there was plenty of room between it and the exit door to complete a FULL CYCLE during our visit. By the way, we offered the ghost all the chocolates and some champagne to make peace. The mirror begins in an upright position (see previous page). It then decides to put itself into other positions. Keep reading.

Art Illustration by Magdalena Adic and Kelly Schutz

HAUNTED MIRROR OR SOMETHING MOVING THE MIRROR?

PRINCE RUPERT SUITE

You can speculate that the MIRROR has loose screws and moves on its own due to walking vibrations and air movement in the room. However, it is also interesting to note that it would ONLY MOVE when my husband passed by it AND wasn't looking at it. Only in my view it would move. The truth be told, the MIRROR had been tightened nearly 10-12 times by me, the assistant manager, and cleaning staff prior to and during our stay.

The ghost loosens its screws on each side (see half way down) with ease and places itself into the position it wants to be in. See images following later in this chapter. You may ask, what caused the MIRROR to cycle round and round? Read my story near the end of this chapter. Slamming of the bathroom door and cycling of the mirror are just two events that occur in The Prince Rupert Suite. Keep reading, more is coming.

HAUNTINGS

What other areas of the hotel are haunted? Everywhere. Although the hauntings occur primarily in the 12th century section of the hotel, no area, including the cellar and newer areas are exempt from a ghostly encounter. There are several ghosts of various ages that roam this building.

1. **ROOM CHANGE.** Upon our arrival, we had a room change from the King James I Suite to the Prince Rupert Suite. We had wanted the Prince Philip Suite, but due its extreme haunted'ness, we were moved to the "next" most haunted.

2. **HALLWAY – STRONG MAGNETIC FIELD.** The reception staff walked with us to our room. As we went up the stairs, located near the reception desk, and made our way on the 2nd floor down a long hallway, one of the reception staff and I felt ourselves walking right into a very strong magnetic field. The field was so strong that it turned both of our faces bright red as a jolt of electricity passed through our bodies. We both commented about how "electrified" we felt from that moment as we reached the Prince Rupert Suite. It was a feeling like no other. Keep reading.

3. **PRINCE PHILIP SUITE – JILTED BRIDE (NO NAME).** A young lady dating back to the Victorian period has a tendency to "hang around" not only in the Prince Philip Suite but out in the hallway. She came to Shrewsbury to be married (date unknown). The day she was due to walk down the aisle, she discovered her husband to-be had run out on her and had married someone else. Mortified, she was so upset that she took her life by hanging herself

from the beams in the Prince Philip Suite, known as Room 5. See next page. She is seen on occasion in that room by unsuspecting guests.

Her hanging body has also appeared in the hallway. The Prince Philip Suite is located in the 12th Century section of the hotel. As reported to me by a hotel cleaning staff person during our stay, the hanging woman does not like the presence of a single man. For example, a painter was in the hallway a few years back working. He was minding his own business painting a wall when the hanging woman decided to appear behind him. Her feet were dangling behind his shoulder. As he caught a glimpse of her out of the corner of his eye, he became bewildered. It is not known if he finished his shift but he did tell a staff person, "I think this place is very sad and I will not be returning." In other words, HE QUIT.

The hung woman also likes to remove bedding and pillows from the bed hiding them in areas out of the room several feet away such as in the elevator lift (60 feet away).

The staff tries to book guests in this room that are not aware of the story behind this haunting.

Photo Taken by Kelly Renee Schutz
Prince Philip Suite, May 27, 2016

PRINCE PHILIP - TABLE AND CHAIRS. To the left, you will notice a table and chairs. It was reported by to me by the Assistant Manager and cleaning staff that on occasion, these chairs are turned around positioned to look OUT the window. This usually occurs after the cleaning staff has just left the room and is noticed by the Assistant Manager. It is as if "THEY" or "SOMEONE" is watching something outside.

PRINCE PHILIP - OBJECTS MOVED. Objects are moved in the room. At times, things are thrown in the room. A heavy feeling and cold breezes are felt.

DAVID BOYCE REPORT. As reported by and transcribed by David Boyce, a clairvoyant who lives in South Wales. On October 8, 2013, he stayed in the Prince Philip Suite a very short time and had an adrenaline rush. He arrived late to the hotel and needed a room. He did not know he would be staying in the most haunted room in the building. In fact, after this discovery and with all that he experienced, he requested a different room in the newer section of the hotel.

VISIONS. As Mr. Boyce was walking to his room, he saw and felt these visions: (a) a fighting and a male in an old uniform being speared in battle; (b) the sense of smoke from an old fire upstairs within the hotel which would have caused significant damage; (c) the feeling that people would have perished or died from smoke inhalation as a result of the fires fumes; (d) a young spirit of a girl wandering the corridors; (e) persons staying in the hotel would complain they smelled residual smoke in areas where none should be; (f) sense of a male who had fallen and tumbled down the stairs in the corridor and died from his injuries; (g) small young girl about

7 years old with long curly hair wearing what looked like an old homemade dress. Small white dog, looks like a Scottie, walking the corridor. Felt Anne might the be the child's name; (h) little girl may have been one of those who passed from smoke inhalation from a fire on the premises,

VISIONS IN PRINCE PHILIP SUITE. As David was in the Prince Philip Suite, he saw these visions: (a) he heard out loud, the name Mary Ellen, being called out by a male from the spirit world as if he were waiting for her to cross over to be with him again. Is this the name of the hanged woman? (b) while sitting on the bed upright with pillows behind him, he felt an intermittent breeze hit his right cheek. He could not determine where it came from and concluded it was not coming from the closed window or through the door that led into the conference area to his right-hand side. Stopped after several minutes; (c) felt constantly nauseas and dizzy with sick churning stomach, feeling as though someone was very nervous; (d) heart rate started racing and breathing became restricted as though someone was pushing on his upper chest; (e) spirit was showing him the gallows in the room near the right of the window as if dropping down to the street outside. Hanging feeling impressed upon him. There was something different to the left-hand side corner of the room as if it was a newer false ceiling.

(f) the name Mr. Hartnell was spoken from the spirit. (g) was shown a portly man who looks about 5'4" tall. He was wearing a waist coat and top hat. He was looking at his pocket watch attached to his waist coat on a chain. He seemed agitated as though he was waiting for someone who was late. He looked like an important person of the time. (h) smell of fresh flowers within the room when there were none anywhere.

Mr. Boyce didn't feel as though the spirits were dangerous or would hurt him. But when they are active, they are strong. A member of the staff had informed him an old original painting was hung on the wall within the present breakfast area prior to the hotel changing hands a few years back. It is believed the painting was sold and no longer within the hotel.

MORE HAUNTS

MY NAME IS MARTHA. According to the writings of Martin Wood, it was during the 1980's when a medium was staying at the hotel. The medium reported that she was going down the spiral staircase into the old kitchen when she had seen a young maid by the name of Martha. Martha had asked why gunshots were fired. The manager at the time knew they had no one working there by that name and stated there was no spiral staircase.

The manager said if gunshots were heard that the entire town would have been alerted. It was until present owner, Mike Matthews took over the hotel, that the discovery of a spiral staircase, constructed around the mid-1700's, that led to the old kitchen was discovered. Matthews had wanted to build a fitness center in that area. When they lifted the floorboards to lay foundation, they discovered a skeleton. The last known maid on record was named Martha. See her image on the next page.

SIDE NOTE: My ability to see ghosts is strengthening. I saw Martha in the hallway as we were walking to our room (Prince Rupert Suite). I caught a glimpse of her face, side view, skin tone as seen on next page, with short brown hair. I was not looking for or paying attention when this blurrrr caught my eye. She was rushing and vanished quickly. Yes, I really saw her.

According to the writings of Martin Wood, Martha was a quiet lady whose shadow was often seen standing in a corner in the kitchen [not clear if it is existing kitchen], just like a maid would have done. He says if you run your hand across the corner about 4 feet above the ground, he says, you can often feel a cold draft as if she is moving away.

Martha has also been seen in the ballroom as an energy orb. It has also been mentioned that when she manifests, she is holding a mop and bucket, as if she were to start cleaning.

Is This Martha, the Hotel Maid?

On the next page, to the right of the crooked stairways is The Prince Rupert Suite, where we stayed. The stairs leading upward go to the Prince Maurice's Suite. One of the cleaning staff told me she does not like going into that room because she feels sick, her energy is immediately drained, and she feels watched. These are symptoms of being attacked. If the entity in this room is angry, it will prey on a fearful person. My advice: (1) wear a cross, (2) say a protection prayer, (3) surround yourself with white light, (4) throw holy water on the floor upon entrance, and (5) ask that the entity not bother you. This may be the area where a fire occurred centuries ago. This room is in the 12th Century manor room section. This is also the area that Martha is seen walking the hallways. To the left, is a set of stairs that leads down to a fitness center. On the fitness center level is a door. Behind that door is a stone carved staircase that leads down into the cellar. Notice the mirror to the right of the stairs? Mirrors are major conductors to manifest hauntings.

PRINCE CHARLES SUITE. Next door to the Prince Philip Suite is the Prince Charles Suite. In a different period of time, a to-be groom took his life in that room when his to-be wife ran off with his best man. A co-worker, who was with David Boyce the evening of his experience, stayed in this room. He reported seeing an apparition appear to him. He didn't say anything to anyone for a long time for fear of being ridiculed.

THE FLANNEL NIGHTSHIRT GHOST. Some years ago, a film of *A Christmas Carol* was being made at Shrewsbury, with several of the film-crew staying at the Prince Rupert Hotel. A director, on his way to bed, saw an elderly man walking towards him wearing a flannel nightshirt. The director stood aside to allow him to pass. The phantom ghost nodded and vanished through a wall carrying a Wee Willy Winkie-type candle holder with a lit candle.

Photo Taken by Kelly Renee Schutz

BAR AREA ACROSS FROM RECEPTION. People have gone to the bar very late at night and upon entering the bar have noticed shadows and a black object hovering above.

ROOM 11. Guests have reported capturing many orbs in motion in this room.

PRINCE MAURICE ROOM. Guests have reported hearing footsteps above them (from Prince Rupert Suite) coming from this room when no one is there. The room is carpeted, which should muffle the sounds of footsteps – but – they are loud and clearly heard.

COLD SPOTS, FEELING WATCHED. Guests have reported seeing a black shadow figure standing next to a window by a conference room. Are they referring to the Prince Philip Suite? Have also reported when attempting to make contact with an apparition in one particular room, would hear Mary Elsbeth. Mary Elsbeth had a child out of wedlock and 2 other children. When asked questions, ghost equipment would respond by flickering. Notice the name is similar to that of David Boyce's report?

KING JAMES SUITE. When a sensitive guest went into this room, she felt that someone who hung about in there "didn't want her there." She did not notice until she walked around the bed the bedding on one side had been turned back. A sign to her, she went to a different room.

ASSISTANT MANAGER. Felt a feeling of something "brushing" on the back of her neck by something when alone working. Turned around and nothing was there.

FOOTSTEPS. Footsteps are heard walking behind staff and guests when no one is in the area or the environment appears peaceful. Some often heard on the 2nd floor.

RESTAURANT. The lights above us were flickering on and off when we ate dinner one evening. We were the only people in the restaurant. No other lights were flickering around us as we had a full view of more than half of the restaurant area and could see all lighting.

CELLAR BOY
Did This Young Boy Lead A Woman Back Safely?

LITTLE BOY, THOMAS. As written by Martin Wood, in the cellar of the Prince Rupert Hotel is the ghost of a small boy, most believe to be named Thomas. This young boy (see picture above) looks as if he dates to the Tudor period.

Many people have spotted Thomas standing by the outer retaining wall. On the other side of that wall, use to be a duck pond. It is alleged Thomas drowned in the Dock Pond. Not, "duck" … "dock" pond. Water from the dock pond would run off down what is known as a dogpole and pass behind the houses on Wyle Cop before entering the river Severn.

WOMAN LOST, HAND HELD. A woman, who became lost on one of the tours, reported that she felt it was Thomas who led her back to a familiar part of the hotel through its confusing hallways. In a mild panic, she felt as though his small hand took ahold of hers and as she tried to "clutch" a fist, was unable to because she felt the shape of a hand inside hers. She then felt herself being led by "someone" back to a familiar part of the building.

SCREAMING BOY. In another incident, not certain if Thomas, guests were awakened one night when they heard sounds of a young boy frantically trying to get into their room. The room reported was Room 1.

He was crying at the top of his lungs and the door knob was moving insinuating that he was trying to be let in or wanted in. When the guests came to the door and opened it, no one was there. His screams were frightening.

STONE CELLAR – TURNED INTO WINE CELLAR

THE CHOKING GHOST. As viewed in the YouTube video, Martin Wood, local historian, was giving a small tour of the cellars when he began talking about the unfriendly, angry man (ghost) who didn't like him or too many people standing in "his" room. On occasion, tourists have heard him telling them "to leave." (they do). This angry man likes to put the feeling of his hands around people's necks (choking). A woman, who was standing at the top of a stairs, squealed as she caught her necklace of green stones before it fell to the floor. The woman said she felt as though someone were unscrewing it. No one was behind her. She left the tour.

KNOCKS ON DOORS. Some guests have reported hearing knocks on their doors only to find no one there. Guests have left their lights and televisions on all evening to drown out any noises they proclaim to hear in their rooms or outside their doors. In my attempt to turn our television on, around 3:30 AM, with our lights on by the way, our remote was dead. Apparitions like to drain the batteries of remote controls. All I can say is, I wish they left ours alone.

WALLPAPER IN ROOM 1. When the wallpaper was being removed in Room1, it was noticed that there would be a lot of ghostly activity. Ghosts do not like change.

HAUNTINGS IN PRINCE RUPERT SUITE

Photo of Prince Rupert
Artwork Displayed in Lobby Near Lift

For those who have stayed in the Prince Rupert Suite and had an experience, I applaud you. My husband and I will never forget our time in this room. This room demonstrated that an 82% moon phase can bring about extreme activity. Or, in this case, it may not matter at all. We stayed in this room on May 27, 2016.

INCIDENTS IN PRINCE RUPERT SUITE

1. As of our visit, this room has 4 mirrors that surround every angle. Ghostly activity thrives with mirrors in a room.

2. Most frequent, the SLAMMING of the bathroom door. Although the entrance leading into the bathroom is sloped downward, this slope is not enough force to slam a door. Ghosts love to slam doors. We placed a luggage rack against it to avoid slamming or shutting.

3. IMAGE in wardrobe mirror no one can figure out.

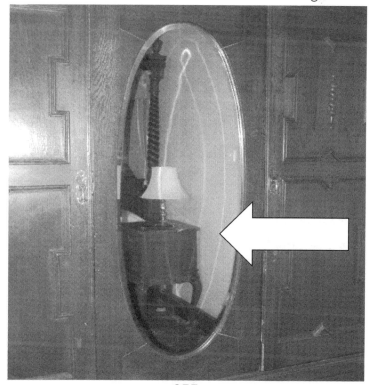

THEORY OF ODD SHAPED LINE. My husband seems to think that this odd marking that follows the oval pattern of the mirror is a reflection of its edges. What you cannot see is that at the bottom, it twists into a hanging noose. Others have captured this image. I have captured it with and without a flash. It projects onto the door that leads into the room. I would be curious to know what the glass is made out of and if there is anything behind that glass to cause this image reflecting outward.

4. Imprints of BUTT on the bed or HANDS on the pillow are common. You can't see them, but the hand prints are on my pillow (left hand side). Husband looks unaffected, huh. Take a look at the REAL ORB that is on the mirror of the wardrobe (to the left). The entity in this room likes to sit on the bed toward the end. Never noticed hand prints.

5. Ghost in this room likes to move the pillows.

6. Ghost in this room does not like the maintenance people coming in, period. When our lamp wasn't working, one had to attempt to go into that room. However, before the ghost lets anyone in, you have to ask permission when entering. My lamp (left side) was not working and it was not clear if it were a bulb issue. I had intended to leave it on all night. When husband and I were at dinner, our key was requested by the assistant manager because the ghost would not let the maintenance person into our room. In fact, the ghost pushes back on the door. Common occurrence. You may be thinking - oh, the maintenance person put his hand prints all over my pillow when he was tampering with the lamp. Nope. You didn't see how the hand prints were displayed on the pillow – like a crime scene.

7. Within 15 minutes of our being in the room, I began having a headache and not feeling 100%. The air felt heavy and it didn't feel right. After walking through the electromagnetic field in the hallway, it was as though my ability to feel or sense spirits was coming to life. I will sequence some pictures for you so you can understand what we (I) went through. When ghosts how themselves, they do not often show to more than one person. Because I am

extremely open, something can happen right in front of you and the other person won't see. Here is a mini-journey of pictures.

ENTERING THE ROOM – NOTICE THE MIRROR STRAIGHT UP. NO HAND PRINTS PILLOWS. NO BUTT PRINT ON BED. AFTER SUPPER, DIFFERENT STORY.

HUSBAND BLESSES THE ROOM WITH HOLY WATER

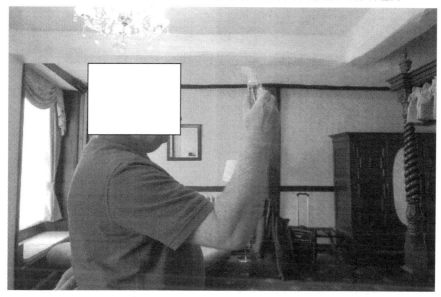

LOOKS CALM AND UNEVENTFUL DOESN'T IT?

NO ACTIVITY, SO IT SEEMS

ACITIVITY BEFORE DINNER – TWO ORBS ON BED

BEFORE DINNER, ORB ON SOFA WAITING PATIENTLY

BEFORE DINNER, ORB NEAR CEILING - SOLID

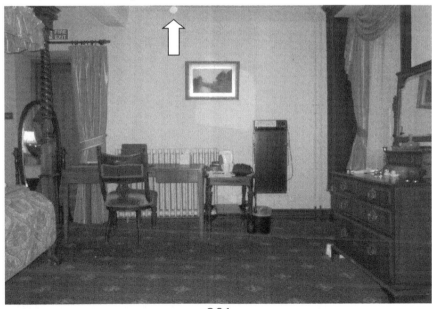

AFTER DINNER, WE FIND THE MIRROR LIKE THIS

BEFORE BED, ORB IS SOLID. HUSBAND UNAFFECTED.

My K2 Meter Never Blinked

BEFORE BED, ORB MOVING AWAY. HUSBAND UNAFFECTED.

SIDE NOTE: When we arrived back from dinner, I have to admit, I was skeptical of the maintenance man. I thought he might have put the hand prints on the pillow and moved the mirror.

MIRROR WAS TIGHTENED. However, this did not happen. The mirror had been tightened several times. Tightened to the point where it could not move easily or at all. However, the ghost didn't like the STRAIGHT UP mirror and kept moving it. When my husband would walk past it, it would move [because he would not see it and I would; no, it wasn't a vibration causing it to move, it almost appeared like a joke to the ghost to do this when he wasn't paying attention]. See image next page.

READY FOR BED – TERROR. At 1:30 PM-2:00 AM, my husband wanted to go to bed. He took the holy water from his dresser and he started to say the IN NAME OF CHRIST protection prayer. I was standing on my side of the bed looking at the mirror. He was standing at the foot of the bed with his body TURNED AWAY from the mirror. As soon as he started saying that prayer, the mirror JOLTED, like a race horse coming out of its gate at a race and began **CYCLING ROUND (Full Circle).** I stood there terrified and looked white (says my husband). When I said, "LOOK" ... it had stopped in the position I am showing you in the next picture.

CYCLING MIRROR. I have video of this mirror moving. From the moment we arrived, I couldn't take my eyes off of the oval mirror. I felt there was something odd about it. Let me remind you that the mirror has been repositioned in this room. In 2012, it was in front of a wall and window on the other side of the room. During our stay, it was positioned in front of an exit door with lots of space behind it to CYCLE. I questioned if ghosts were coming and going through the exit door moving the mirror. I questioned if that oval mirror, which directly faces the wardrobe, had double the power to manifest ghostly entities. I had questioned if someone had taken a strong possession over that room finding comfort in sitting and sleeping on the bed. Mirrors absorb energy. What is its story?

THIS IS HOW THE MIRROR LIKES ITS POSITION

TERRIFED COULDN'T SLEEP. I put a black mask over my face because the incident threw me into a very severe panic attack. I was burning up, red in the face, labored breathing. I hate to even admit this, but the ghost was hovering over my face for several minutes and its "freezing" temperature helped me to settle down a little and feel better. I just asked it wouldn't hurt me. My husband was snoring the entire time. Typical of ghost experiences. Reports have also stated that people would feel a cool breeze over their face or something blowing gently into their ear. I fell asleep around 4:00 AM ... I gave up and passed out.

THE WARDROBE. The wardrobe in that room, that has the strange image in its glass, is a very old piece. In 2012, during the news reporting tour of that room, it was behind the sofa. When we were there, it was facing the oval mirror. The wardrobe is not loose enough to open by itself. You will see in looking at it (next page), that it was open about 1" when I woke up the next day.

With 4 hours of sleep, for some reason, it is possible the ghost sleeps or resides in the wardrobe. When the orb was in the mirror and leaving it (see previous images), the door was closed.

CANDLESTICK. The gold candlestick was moved to an odd position on the dresser with mirror.

TRIGGER OBJECTS. None of my trigger objects were touched or moved.

MANAGEMENT AND CLEANING STAFF. Were brought in the next day and shown what the mirror had done in front of me [us]. I was in error in my report about which side of the mirror was actually "up" – cork down, mirror up. The cleaning staff told both of us that she had been having incidents with the mirror in the past few days. Every time she would straighten it or was bent over, it would hit her. Hit her where? Where do you think? Do you think offering a chocolate matters to the apparition(s) in the room?

BOOK 1

BOOK 1. 235 Pages. **Topics** = Death, Superstitions, Ghost Attractions, Hauntings. **Personal Stories** = 12 Illustrated Real-Life Stories. **Bonus** = Investigator Theoretical Tool Kit, Equipment, and Debunking Paranormal Experiences.

BOOK 2

BOOK 2. 254 Pages. **Topics** = Angels, Demons, Ghost Animals, Portals. **Personal Stories** = 12 Illustrated Real-Life Stories. **Bonus** = Investigator Theoretical Tool Kit, Equipment, and Debunking Paranormal Experiences.

BOOK 3

BOOK 3. 306 Pages. There are NO topics in this book. This book combines together 24 stories from Book 1 and Book 2. **Bonus** = Investigator Theoretical Tool Kit, Equipment, and Debunking Paranormal Experiences.

BOOK 4

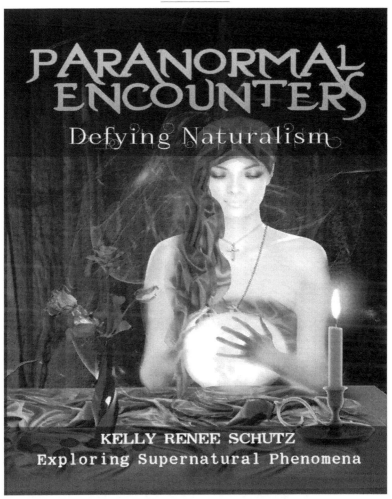

BOOK 4. 202 Pages. **Topics** = Dreams, Near Death, Death, Superstitions, Angels, Demons, Ghost Animals, Psychics, Ghost Attractions, Hauntings, Moon Phases and Energy Fields, Orbs and Vortexes, Portals, Spectral Sites. **Bonus** = Investigator Theoretical Tool Kit, Equipment, and Debunking Paranormal Experiences.

BOOK 5

BOOK 5. 318 Pages. This book contains 5 fiction (not real) and 20 non-fiction (real) paranormal stories. **Bonus** = Debunking Paranormal Experiences.

BOOK 6

BOOK 6. 160 Pages. This book contains fiction, non-fiction, and children perspectives on their ghost experiences. **Bonus** = Adult Stories and Debunking Paranormal Experiences.   373

BOOK 7

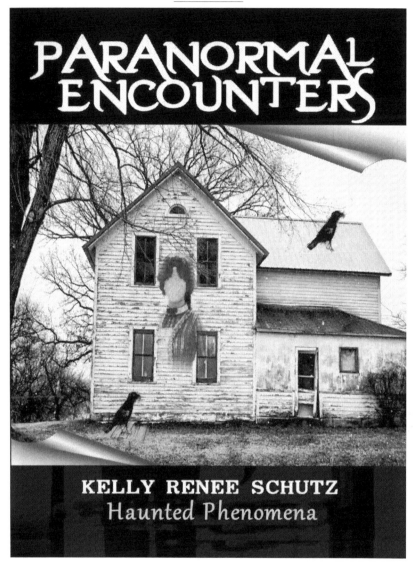

BOOK 7. 200 Pages. This book compiles all stories from Books 1-6 (short versions). 70+ non-fiction paranormal experiences. **Bonus** = Debunking Paranormal Experiences.   374

Paranormal Encounters Podcast Series

Podcasts and Worldwide Interviews

SUBSCRIBE FOR FREE

http://krschutz1paranormalencounters.podomatic.com

OR www.paranormaluniveralpress.com

The Paranormal Encounters Podcast Series (see links above), would not have been as mysterious as it sounded if it were not for the talented music composers who scored original music behind the voices. My voice talents varied but special credit needs to be given to Elliot Shulman, New Jersey, my announcer. Thank you.

Music Composer
Vitaliy Hava, Burshtyn City, Ukraine

Vitaliy Hava resides in Burshtyn City, Ukraine. He has more than 10 years of experience in audio production as a freelancer and has worked with clients all over the globe on original soundtracks for computer games, cartoons, music for television, podcasts, music albums, and radio commercials. He had worked for Garbuz Studio, where he had a chance to master his skills on audio production while delivering high quality projects under strict deadlines. He currently owns his own studio. Contact him thru **upwork.com or vitaliy.hava@gmail.com.**

Music Composer
Evgeny Ryabovol, Kherson, Ukraine

Evgeny Ryabovol resides in Kherson, Ukraine. He studied hydrotechnology at Kherson Agricultural University and earned a diploma as an expert engineer. He became interested in music around the age of 15, initially as a hobby. In 2005, he had a metal-band in which he was the lead singer and guitarist. After five years, the band broke up and Evgeny went on to write and compose music where he has worked to master the principles of sound recording, mixing, mastering and sound design. Contact him thru **upwork.com**.

Music Composer
Jonatan Alberto Arriaga Zaragoza
Mexico City, Mexico

Jonatan Alberto Arriaga Zaragoza resides just outside of Mexico City, Mexico. He has more than five years of experience with sound design and music composition, particularly for the media and songwriting. He loves to score cinematic cues and has experience working with sampled instruments through Native Instruments´ Kontakt. He enjoys creating sounds and music for video games. Currently, he is taking a certification course for WWise middleware. He may be contacted **thru upwork.com.**

Music Composer
Elliott McLaughlin, London, England

Elliott McLaughlin resides in London, England. He is a UK based composer, producer, and songwriter for CLIMBR, featuring contemporary, memorable, and exquisitely polished compositions. He has explored music since an early age. Studied at the Leeds College of Music. From live band multi-instrumentalist, to composer, producer, and DJ, CLIMBR is on a journey to triumph every challenge that music has to offer. A prestigious degree in music production along with years of professional experience, CLIMBR is versatile, dynamic and forward-thinking producer with an expert standard of composition and engineering. Contact him thru **upwork.com**.

Music Composer
Franco Luciano Donatti
Buenos Aires, Argentina

Franco Luciano Donatti resides in Buenos Aires, Argentina. He started to play the piano at the age of 15 years old. Around 2012, he has studied the mastery of arts, a degree in piano at the Buenos Aires National Conservatory. From 2015, he has been studying musical composition at the University of Arts in Buenos Aires. He has composed several music compositions for audiovisuals and video games as well as recorded piano music as a sideman musician. He is currently creating his studio called "Techno Classics1", which aims to create audio production for film scores, video games music, and audio recordings. Contact him thru **upwork.com**.

Music Composer
Phil Michalski, Manchester, United Kingdom

Phil Michalski was born in Warsaw, Poland. He currently resides in Manchester, United Kingdom. In 2007, he graduated from the Academy of Film and TV with a major in sound engineering. Since then, he had worked for the biggest radio station in Poland, "Poland National Radio," as a producer, sound engineer, and composer. In 2013, he moved to the United Kingdom and established a small post production business called AudioPhil, where he currently works as a senior producer for a multiple parsec award-winning podcast, the *NoSleep* podcast. Phil's passion is sound design. He loves to record everything that makes a sound and processes his recording into new sounds. Contact him thru **http://philmichalski.com or upwork.com**.

Made in the USA
Middletown, DE
13 August 2019